THE HOLY SPIRIT OF GOD

By

Richard Rogers

Instructor
Sunset International Bible Institute

SUNSET
INSTITUTE PRESS
3710 34th Street • Lubbock, Texas • 79410
800-687-2121 • www.extensionschool.com

The Holy Spirit of God
© Sunset Institute Press

Copyright © May 2007
Sunset Institute Press

ISBN: 0-9768698-8-8

Printed and Bound in the
United States of America
All Rights Reserved

Cover Design: Richard Cravy
Formatting and Editing: Virgil Yocham

CONTENTS

APPENDICES

PREFACE

This work is an attempt to exalt and enthrone the often-neglected third person of the Godhead, the Holy Spirit of God.

Several of the conclusions reached in this work are directly opposed to the positions held by some of my brethren. I do not differ for difference's sake. I am not trying to be new or original. I *am* trying to be scripturally sound and correct. I do appeal for an honest, open-minded consideration of the exegesis presented. The controversy about various facets of the Spirit's work is not new. I believe two quotations from Lard's Quarterly of over a century ago not only establish this fact but show the proper attitude toward it. The first one is from the pen of J. W. McGarvey:

> An article in the last number of the Quarterly entitled "Baptism in One Spirit Into One Body" has struck the public mind as quite a novelty in the literature of Reformation. It is not only novel, but it is contradictory to some conclusions very generally received among us, and upon a subject which the brethren have studied with great diligence. Of this the author was fully conscious and, in anticipation of the reception which awaited his article, very justly remarked that 'no view is to be rejected merely because it is new.' The lover of truth should never be a dogmatist nor conclude that on any subject he has nothing more to learn. But he should stand ready, whenever his conclusions, even those of which he is most confident, are challenged upon the basis of new reasons, because the mere reiteration of old and oft refuted arguments against any proposition can impose

no such obligation . . . I have for some years been convinced that the immersion in the Holy Spirit is not fully understood, and that it needs investigation and discussion *de novo.* The same may be said of the entire subject of the Holy Spirit and his work in human salvation. Although there are some propositions upon this subject which are well defined, and well settled among us, yet on no other subject are there so many points in which we feel distinctly and painfully the want of certainty.[1]

From the beginning "new"

The next year, Thomas Munnell wrote,

The sensation produced by the appearance of an article in the March issue of the Quarterly, on the Baptism of the Holy Spirit, has been equaled only by that experienced by the agitation of the Communion question during the past two years. The writer of said article should be credited both for originality, boldness, and caution. He neither dogmatizes as to his views, nor falters in expressing them. He does not write as a sensationalist; but as a seeker of truth. All who have capacity enough to admit that some of our views on this subject may have been erroneous, will no doubt be benefitted in reading the discussion; those who are too weak to make such admission would do as well to spend their time some other way. The world has always had its men who, too weak to discuss fairly, have spent their little force in denouncing. This has always been the unfailing source of division among good people; for the reformer, never desiring to leave the church to which he belonged, but to reform it, has nevertheless been uniformly driven out

---

[1] See Appendix for more comments by McGarvey

of the church because of his newly-developed truths. This was the case with Luther, Wesley, Campbell, and all others such as these. Let us, then, never be chargeable with an imbecility that disqualifies us for a reinvestigation of any subject that fairly commands our attention.[2]

There are several people who will not benefit from a study of the Holy Spirit of God. *First,* those who have a steel-trap mind that has already sprung. If your mind is already made up, nothing in this study, or any other, is going to benefit you. *Second,* those who believe we have to defend all statements made by and positions held by the great brethren of the past. Sometimes we are more tradition-bound than all the Romanists Catholicism has produced. *Third,* those who do not want the peace disturbed. The truth has always been disturbing. After Josiah had made all his great religious reforms, purging the land of its idolatry, he was greatly disturbed when the law was read to him because he saw that he had not yet restored the worship of Jehovah in truth and spirit (2 Chronicles 34:19). It was not the truth, but a failure to understand and follow the truth, that disturbed the peace of Israel (I Kings 18:17-18).

Then, who should benefit from a study concerning the Holy Spirit of God? *First,* those who wish a deeper motivation for their spiritual lives. When one realizes the power of the indwelling Spirit, a life of service becomes the spiritual response. *Second,* those willing to accept any truth that the Bible teaches at face value. *Third,* those who enjoy a deep, detailed study of the word of God. These thoughts are not presented as a final answer to anything but rather as an appeal and guide to further study of this grand theme. Study the thoughts presented. Add to them from your own study and let us share your thoughts also.

----

[2] For further discussion on this see the Appendix.

Those to whom I am indebted for thoughts found in this book are legion. I am sure that whoever said "all knowledge is derived" had me in mind. Propriety dictates that acknowledgments be given to a few. (A list of sources consulted in making this study can be found in the Bibliography at the conclusion of this work). Gratitude is first of all expressed to the students of Sunset School of Preaching (now Sunset International Bible Institute), where these lessons were first given, for listening as this material was being developed, and for making invaluable contributions to its content. Appreciation must go to Jim McGuiggan from North Ireland for his useful and outstanding work on "Ye Shall be Baptized With the Holy Spirit" and to Hardeman Nichols for his material on "The Intercession of the Spirit." But ultimately all praise must go to the Father, who not only revealed his will through the Spirit (I Corinthians 2:6-13), but also gave us "a spirit of wisdom and revelation in the knowledge of Him" (Ephesians 1:17). Any blame for mistakes should be credited to the author and to none of his sources.

The grace of our Lord Jesus Christ, and the love of God, and the communion of the Holy Spirit, be with you all.

Richard Rogers
Sunset International Bible Institute
Lubbock, Texas

THE HOLY SPIRIT OF GOD: A PERSON

Introduction

There is a tremendous amount of confusion in the world today concerning the Holy Spirit. Some believe that the Spirit must operate in some mysterious manner upon their heart before they can believe the Word and obey God. Others do not believe that the Spirit, personally, has any active part in their conversion. Some do not even believe the Spirit to be an entity possessing personality, but just a mere influence or principle. Others, while believing the Spirit to be a personality, practically strip Him of any vestige of Deity. These are only a few of the countless positions held by honest people concerning the Holy Spirit of God. This chapter will address itself to the task of answering these two questions: Is the Holy Spirit God? Is the Holy Spirit a person? a living entity? a personality?

The scarcity of material on the Holy Spirit found in brotherhood writings indicates the scarcity of thinking that has been done among us on this, the grandest of subjects. The **popular concept** of the Godhead can best be illustrated by these three circles.

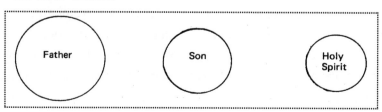

Although we would deny believing in degrees of Godhood, we convict ourselves of such in our thinking on the Holy Spirit. We have no difficulty with the Father. We attribute everything the Bible says about Godhood to Him, and rightly so. We attribute nearly the same deity to the Son. But when we come to the Holy Spirit, we merely relegate Him to the office of messenger boy.

The traditional position can be stated in this way: When Christ went back to heaven, He sent the Spirit to reveal the word unto the apostles. The Spirit also worked miraculously in them and in those upon whom the apostles laid their hands. Having done those two things, the Spirit returned to Heaven, His work accomplished. So we have taught, in essence, for several generations.

The following diagram with three circles comes much closer to presenting the Biblical doctrine of the Godhead.

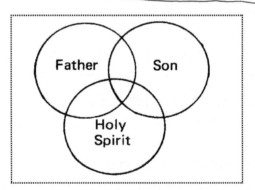

Since all three – The Father, The Son and The Holy Spirit – are Deity, the circles must be of equal size. Since their works are too interrelated to ever be separated, the circles must be drawn interlocking. Indeed one of them may have a work which is His alone, but in the majority of the cases, there is perfect cooperation of all three, in each and every work that Godhood does.

The Holy Spirit Is a Person

This can be seen from at least three separate viewpoints.

The Works of The Holy Spirit
Manifest His Personality

The Holy Spirit is a Divine Person. He possesses the attributes of personality (John 16:13-14). Nine times He is spoken of as a Person. He is life, thought, volition, action, speech, individuality, character and influence.

He Speaks: and He empowered the apostles to speak (Acts 2). In I Timothy 4:1 Paul says, *"The Spirit saith expressly, that in later times some shall fall away from the faith."*

He Witnesses: *"But when the comforter is come, whom I will send unto you from the Father, even the Spirit of truth, which proceedeth from the Father, he shall bear witness of me"* (John 15:26).

He Teaches: *"But the Comforter, even the Holy Spirit, whom the Father will send in my name, he shall teach you all things, and bring to your remembrance all that I said unto you"* (John 14:26).

He Guides: *"Howbeit when he, the Spirit of truth, is come, he shall guide you unto all the truth"* (John 16:13). These are characteristics of a Divine Person, who possesses intelligence.

He Leads and Forbids: In Acts 16:6-10, Luke records a very interesting occurrence in the life of the Apostle Paul. Paul was forbidden by the Holy Spirit to speak the word in Asia. He wanted to go into Bithynia but the Spirit would not permit it. He passed on to Troas, where in a vision by night he received a call to come into Macedonia. The Spirit had thus forbidden him to preach in Asia and Bithynia and had led him to preach in Macedonia.

*THESE WORKS COULD NOT BE ATTRIBUTED TO A
MERE INFLUENCE. THE HOLY SPIRIT IS A PERSON.*

The Characteristics of the Holy Spirit
Declare His Personality

He Possesses Mind. In Romans 8:27 Paul says, *"He that searches the hearts knoweth what is the mind of the Spirit."*

He Has Knowledge*: "For who among men knoweth the things of a man, save the spirit of the man, which is in him? Even so the things of God none knoweth, save the Spirit of God"* (I Corinthians 2:1 1).

He Has Affections*:* The highest of all affections is attributed to the Spirit. *"Now I beseech you, brethren, by our Lord Jesus Christ, and by the love of the Spirit, that ye strive together with me in your prayers to God for me"* (Romans 15:30).

He Possesses a Will*: "But all these worketh the one and the same Spirit, dividing to each one severally even as he will"* (I Corinthians 12:11).

THESE ARE ALL CHARACTERISTICS OF A PERSON.
THE HOLY SPIRIT IS AN ENTITY POSSESSING
INTELLIGENCE.

The Slights and Injuries Suffered
Declare His Personality

He Can Be Grieved*: "Grieve not the Holy Spirit of God, in whom ye were sealed unto the day of redemption"* (Ephesians 4:30). Compare Isaiah 63: 10.

He Can Be Resisted: *"Ye stiff-necked and uncircumcised in heart and ears, ye do always resist the Holy Spirit"* (Acts 5:3).

He Can Be Blasphemed*: "Whosoever shall speak against the Holy Spirit, it shall not be forgiven him, neither in this world, nor in that which is to come"* (Matthew 12:32).

ONLY A PERSONALITY CAN BE TREATED IN THIS MATTER. THE HOLY SPIRIT IS A PERSON.

The Holy Spirit Is a Person of Deity
He Is God

This, too, can be proven from three separate viewpoints.

The Holy Spirit Possesses the Attributes of Deity

He is Eternal: *"How much more shall the blood of Christ, who through the eternal Spirit offered himself without blemish, cleanse your conscience from dead works to serve the living God"* (Hebrews 9:14).

He is Omniscient. *"The Spirit searcheth all things, yea, the deep things of God"* (I Corinthians 2:10).

He is Omnipotent: *"But as for me, I am full of power by the Spirit of Jehovah, and of judgment and of might, to declare unto Jacob his transgression, and to Israel his sin"* (Micah 3:8).

He is Omnipresent: *"Whither shall I go from thy Spirit? Or whither shall I flee from thy presence? If I ascend up into heaven, thou art there! If I make my bed in Sheol, behold, thou art there. If I take the wings of the morning and dwell in the uttermost parts of the sea, even there thy hand shall lead me, and thy right hand shall hold me"* (Psalms 139:7-10).

The Holy Spirit Does the Works of Deity

He Created the Universe.: *"Thou sendest forth thy Spirit, they are created; and thou renewest the face of the ground"* (Psalms 104:30).

He Regenerates Man: *"Verily, verily, I say unto thee, except one be born of water and the Spirit, he cannot enter into the kingdom of God"* (John 3:5).

He Will Resurrect the Body: *"He that raised up Jesus from the dead shall give life also to your mortal bodies through his Spirit that dwelleth in you"* (Romans 8:11).

He Performed Miracles: In I Corinthians 12:4-11, Paul lists the miraculous gifts that were present in the first century. He concludes that these all came because of the Spirit.

A Study of the Godhead Reveals That the Spirit Is Deity

At the Baptism of Jesus, we find all three persons in the Godhead manifested: Jesus, the son of God, the Holy Spirit of God descending in bodily form as a dove, and the voice of the Father, *"Thou art my beloved son; in thee I am well pleased"* (Luke 3:21-22).

Jesus Speaks of the Three (John 14:16-17). *"I* (Jesus) *will pray the Father and he will send the Comforter* (Holy Spirit).*"*

The Authority of all three is Invoked at Baptism (Matthew 28:18-20). *". . .in the name of the Father and the Son and the Holy Spirit."*

The Assurance of the Godhead (Romans 8:12-17). The *Father* gives us the *Spirit of* adoption and we become heirs with Christ.

Paul's Great Benediction (2 Corinthians 13:14). *"The grace of the Lord Jesus Christ; and the love of God; and the communion of Holy Spirit."*

Greetings from the Eternal Godhead, Revelation 1:4-5

1. Him who is, was and is to come–The Father.
2. Seven Spirits before His Throne–Holy Spirit.
3. The Faithful Witness–Jesus Christ.

BY THE COMPANY THAT HE KEEPS WE KNOW THAT THE HOLY SPIRIT IS A PERSON IN THE ETERNAL GODHEAD. HE IS A PERSON. HE IS GOD.

SUMMARY

The fact that the Holy Spirit is revealed in the Bible to be a person and a member of the eternal Godhead makes this an important subject. With all the search that man can do, he has not been able to discover anything of the nature of the Godhead except what he finds in the Bible. Therefore, it is to this Book of books that we will turn to find answers to all of our questions about the Holy Spirit of God.

QUESTIONS

Chapter One

1.   Richard says there is a scarcity of material in the brotherhood about the Holy Spirit. Why do you think this is the case?

2.   What is the traditional position of many Christians today concerning the relationship between God the Father, Jesus Christ and the Holy Spirit?

3.   Name at least five works of the Holy Spirit which manifests His personality.

4.   Discuss four characteristics of the Holy Spirit which declare His personality.

5.   Would you be able to convince someone the Holy Spirit is deity? How would you go about doing this? What evidence would you present?

6.   What things about the Godhead would indicate the Holy Spirit is deity?

Chapter Two

THE HOLY SPIRIT OF GOD: ACTIVE IN THE OLD TESTAMENT

Introduction

The difference between the Spirit's activity in the Old Testament and His activity in the New Testament is best seen in John 14:17: *"Even the Spirit of Truth; whom the world cannot receive; for it beholdeth him not, neither knoweth him; ye know him; for he abideth **with** you, and shall be **in** you."* In the Old Testament the Holy Spirit was "with" them, empowering them, guiding them. In the New Testament the Spirit is "in" them, indwelling them, sealing them as sons, etc. This difference is something which we will need to keep in mind in this study.

The Spirit's activity in the Old Testament is not as clearly outlined as in the New Testament. But in the passages that deal with His work, we notice two distinct realms in which He is active: in the natural creation and in the theocratic nation.

The Natural Creation

All three members of the Godhead were active in the creation. The Father planned, purposed, and originated all things (Revelation 4:11). The Word or Christ was the agent of creation (John 1:1-3; Colossians 1:16; Hebrews 1:2). The Holy Spirit organized, gave laws for, and today guides the physical universe. (See proof below.)

The Spirit had a special activity in creation as expressed in Genesis 1:2, "*And the earth was waste and void; and darkness was upon the face of the deep: and the Spirit of God moved upon* (brooded upon, mg) *the face of the waters.*" The translation "moved" or "brooded" literally means "to be anxious over, to be tremulous, as with love." This indicates the Spirit's anxiety to get to work and bring order out of chaos. Thus, in this, the first mention of the Holy Spirit of God, we already have an indication of the nature of the Holy Spirit and His work. He is the Order-bringer. In Psalms 104:30 David said that God sent forth the Spirit to renew the face of the ground. "*When you send your Spirit, they are created, and you renew the face of the earth.*" (NIV)

The Spirit is also the source of judgment for the things created, "*When the enemy shall come in like a flood, the Spirit of the LORD shall lift up a standard against him.*" (Isaiah 59:19 (KJV.); 40:12-14.) In Psalms 139:7-10 David has great faith in the all-inclusiveness of the providence of God because of the omnipresence of the Holy Spirit.

The Theocratic Nation

In the Theocratic Nation we see the Holy Spirit as the source of all supernatural powers and activities which are directed to the foundation, preservation and development of the Kingdom of God in the midst of the wicked world.

As great as the power of the Spirit was in creation, and is in governing and guiding the things created, His power in the history of Israel is greater.

Moses was the great leader of Israel because of the Spirit which was upon him (Numbers 11:16-17). Joshua was singled out as successor to Moses because he was a man of the Spirit (Numbers 27:18).

The book of Judges is a book of warfare and bloodshed. Yet, at the same time, hardly any book in the Bible exalts the Holy Spirit of God more than Judges. When Israel needed deliverance from Mesopotamia, Othniel arose and the Spirit came upon him (Judges 3:10). Later, when Midian oppressed Israel, the Spirit clothed himself with Gideon. "*But the Spirit of the LORD came upon Gideon. . .*" (Judges 6:34). Similarly, Jephthah was empowered (Judges 11:29). Samson's strength was not in his hair but in the Spirit (Judges 13:25; 14:6; 19:15:14). In these passages we notice that before every great deed of strength and valor, the Spirit of Jehovah came mightily upon Samson. When he was unfaithful to God and to his Nazarite vow and allowed his hair to be cut, the Spirit left him (cf. Judges 16:20).

When the nation was established and Saul was selected to be king, Samuel anointed him with oil (1 Samuel 10:1). And then in verse 6, he prophesied that the Spirit of Jehovah would come upon him. In the next chapter we read, "*And the Spirit of God came mightily upon Saul*" (1 Samuel 11:6). God had anointed him with the Holy Spirit. When David was anointed by Samuel, the Spirit of Jehovah came upon him from that day forward (1 Samuel 16:13). The only true leader for God's nation is a man of the Spirit. The conviction of the Old Testament is that no man can do the work of God without the Spirit. No man is worthy to lead his fellow-men unless led by the Spirit of God. Without the Spirit, no amount of intellectual power, no amount of administrative ability, not even the capacity to toil, will suffice.

In the Old Testament the prominent gift of the Holy Spirit was supernatural knowledge culminating in prophecy. The Spirit gave the prophet Balaam his message (Numbers 24:2). It was by the Spirit that was upon Moses that the seventy elders temporarily prophesied (Numbers 11:25). "*The Spirit of*

Jehovah spake by me, and his word was upon my tongue," said David in 2 Samuel 23:2. Isaiah claimed, *"The Lord Jehovah hath sent me, and His Spirit"* (48:16). The word from the Spirit through the prophet might be one of comfort, of consolation, of promise, of threat, or of condemnation; but it was always a sure word. Men disregarded that prophetic word at their own peril. In Zechariah 7:8-14, the people of Israel were told to repent or perish. They refused to heed the word of Zechariah as they had refused to heed the word of the former prophets. Because of this, God said that He would not hear them when they prayed and that He would scatter them with a whirlwind among all the nations. Micah 3:8 could be called the climactic passage on the Spirit's power over the prophets. *"But as for me, I am full of power by the Spirit of Jehovah, and of judgment and of might, to declare unto Jacob his transgression and to Israel his sin."* The Spirit of Jehovah gave Ezekiel his commission and his message. *"And the Spirit entered into me when he spake unto me and set me upon my feet"* (2:2). It is the consistent teaching of the Old Testament that no man could prophesy without the Spirit of Jehovah. It was the Spirit of Jehovah that gave the prophet the power to bring God's word to man, whether the message was one of consolation or condemnation.

Preeminently, in the Old Testament, Israel was a nation in the midst of which the Holy Spirit of God dwelt.

> *But they rebelled and grieved his holy Spirit . . . Then he remembered the days of old, Moses and His people, saying, "'Where is he that brought them up out of the sea with the shepherds of His flock? Where is he that put his Holy Spirit in the midst of them?" As the cattle that go down into the valley, the Spirit of Jehovah caused them to rest: so didst thou lead thy people, to make thyself a glorious name"* (Isaiah 63:10-14).

In Haggai's short book, God tells the remnant of Israel if they would build the temple, then He would be with them as he had covenanted when He led them out of Egypt. *"And my Spirit abode among you, fear ye not* (2:4-5).

One feature of the Spirit's work for the nation of Israel that is rather unique is the gift of craftsmanship. It is not hard for us to see the need of the Spirit in order to perform miracles or to prophesy. But, because Israel had been slaves in Egypt for over 400 years, they had no skilled craftsmen to build the tabernacle. So we read in Exodus 31:1-5,

> *And Jehovah spake unto Moses, saying "See, I have called by name Bezalel . . . and I have filled him with the Spirit of God, in wisdom, and in understanding, and in knowledge, and in all manner of workmanship, to devise skillful works, to work in gold, and in silver, and in brass, and in cutting of stones for setting, and in carving of wood, to work in all manner of workmanship."*

This takes the work of the Spirit out of the realm of religious activity alone and puts Him in the shop, in the mill, in the office. This is also New Testament teaching. In Romans 12 Paul discusses gifts that the Spirit gives men.

> *And having gifts differing according to the grace that was given to us, whether prophecy, let us prophesy according to the proportion of our faith; or ministry, let us give ourselves to our ministry, or he that teacheth to his teaching; or he that exhorteth to his exhorting.*

It is not hard to see how each of these come to man through the Spirit. But notice the next gift. *"He that giveth, let him do it with liberality."* The single-minded giving of money is listed by Paul as a gift of the Spirit right along with prophesying, etc.

We can summarize the activity of the Holy Spirit of God in the Old Testament as follows:

1. He appeared in Creation (Genesis 1:2; Psalms 104:30).
2. He appeared in revealing dreams (Genesis 41:15, 38).
3. He gave prophetic vision (Numbers 24:2; Micah 3:8).
4. He gave power to the rulers (Judges 6:34; 1 Samuel 16:13).
5. He revealed himself in workmanship (Exodus 31:1-5).

QUESTIONS

Chapter Two

1. What difference is seen in the activity of the Holy Spirit in the Old Testament and in the New Testament?

2. In what two areas was the Holy Spirit involved in the Old Testament?

3. Since the prominent gift of the Holy Spirit in the Old Testament was supernatural knowledge, how did this relate to prophecy and prophets?

4. Since the Holy Spirit gifted craftsmen in the Old Testament, can we expect Him to be involved in like activity today? Does Romans 12 say anything about this?

5. Summarize the activity of the Holy Spirit in the Old Testament.

Chapter Three

THE HOLY SPIRIT OF GOD AND THE WRITTEN WORD

Introduction

What does the Bible teach concerning the relation of the Spirit and the written word of God? What is the Spirit's relation to revelation and inspiration? Are the Word of God and the Spirit of God one and the same thing? Does the Spirit have any work in salvation, sanctification, comfort, and glorification that He does immediately (i.e. without medium), or does He do all of these things through the written word? These and other questions will be discussed and answered in this chapter.

The primary concern of the Holy Spirit is to bring man to God and to reveal God to man. The Holy Spirit of God is therefore the author of the Word of Life, the Sacred Scriptures, God's unerring revelation to man.

Revelation.

God has revealed Himself to man in various ways. At first, in the garden of Eden, God spoke directly to Adam and Eve (Genesis 3:8ff). Noah was given personal instructions in order to escape the coming judgement by God upon the wicked world in the Flood (Genesis 6:13ff). The patriarchs Abraham, Isaac, and Jacob were personally comforted by the divine promise of their seed becoming the means for a world-wide blessing

(Genesis 12:1-3; 22:18; 26:1-6; 28:3-4; 13-14). It was the audible voice of Jehovah that spoke to Moses out of the burning bush in Midian and told him to go back to Egypt and deliver the people out of bondage (Exodus 3).

God has also revealed Himself in His creation, in the physical world in which we live day by day. It is as David sang in the nineteenth Psalm,

> *The heavens declare the glory of God; and the firmament showeth his handiwork. Day unto day uttereth speech, and night unto night showeth knowledge. There is no speech nor language; where their voice is not heard. Their line is gone out through all the earth, and their words to the end of the world* (Psalm 19:1-4).

So evident is this revelation of Himself in creation that Paul concludes this makes those who would deny the existence of God inexcusable:

> *For the wrath of God is revealed from heaven against all ungodliness and unrighteousness; because that which is known of God is manifest in them; for God manifested it unto them. For the invisible things of him since the creation of the world are clearly seen, being perceived through the things that are made, even his everlasting power and divinity; that they might be without excuse* (Romans 1:18-20).

Existence, order, design, and purpose in the physical world testify to the wisdom, glory and power of God who is the creator of it all.

God also revealed the exact *nature* of His invisible attributes through the eternal Word, Jesus Christ. In his life, death, and resurrection, Jesus reveals to man what God is like and what God would have man to be. In Christ the invisible God becomes visible to the wandering eyes of those who would love God.

> *In the beginning was the Word, and the Word was with God, and the Word was God . . . And the Word became flesh, and dwelt among us (and we beheld his glory, glory as of the only begotten of the Father), full of grace and truth . . . No man hath seen God at any time; the only begotten Son, who is in the bosom of the Father, he hath declared* (exegeted) *him* (John 1:1, 14, 18).

In this section, however, we will be chiefly concerned with the written word, God's permanent and definite revelation to man. We want to notice specifically the origin, revelation, preservation, inspiration, authority and power of the written word; and, in detail, the work of the Spirit in this regard.

Revelation and Inspiration

In order to proceed with clearness and dispatch, we must understand what revelation and inspiration are. Revelation is the action of God that enables man to know the unknowable (i.e. what he cannot discern through his own senses and abilities). Inspiration is that action of God upon man that enables him to inerrantly record this revelation for the good of mankind. All scripture is the result of inspiration (2 Timothy 3:16), but not everything recorded by inspiration is a matter of revelation.

The historical accounts contained in Kings and Chronicles did not need to be revealed. They were matters of history. The recording of these for our learning, however, was a matter of divine inspiration. That there was a place in Judah named Bethlehem was a matter of geographic fact, but that the

Messiah was to be born in this obscure village was a matter of both revelation and inspiration (Micah 5:2). Many of the words of Job and his "friends" are the twisted reflections of men who did not understand God's nature. However, these words are recorded by inspiration for our admonition and instruction.

In the Old Testament, God revealed portions of His will to men, both good and evil. Balaam, the materialist, spoke by the Spirit (Numbers 24:2). Even his donkey, a dumb beast, was enabled by God to speak. In Moses the activity of a prophet comes into full display. God spoke to him repeatedly and finally said, "*I will raise them up a prophet from among their brethren, like unto thee; and I will put my words in his mouth, and he shall speak unto them all that I shall command him*" (Deuteronomy 18:18).

After Israel inherited the land of promise the office of prophecy became more and more prominent. Schools of prophets arose (1 Samuel 19:18-21, *et al).* And with the rise of the kings, the office of prophet reached its full fruit in such men as Amos, Hosea, Micah, Isaiah, Zephaniah, and Jeremiah. Upon the return from Babylonian captivity, God raised up Haggai and Zechariah to encourage the people in the re-building of the temple. And finally Malachi cries out against the people's idleness and indifference.

The Spirit and Revelation

What part does the Spirit play in the revelation of God's will? Peter presents us with the key to this question: "*For no prophecy ever came by the will of man: but men spake from God, being moved by the Holy Spirit*" (2 Peter 1:21). The source of prophecy, according to Peter is God, and furthermore, is attributed to the influence of the Spirit upon men, bearing them from one place to another as a moving van transports furniture from one city to another.

This statement from Peter is borne out by the experiences of men of the Spirit. In Numbers 11:25 the Spirit that was upon Moses was placed upon the seventy elders and they prophesied. When Joshua wanted Moses to forbid this, Moses said, *"Would that all Jehovah's people were prophets, that Jehovah would put His Spirit upon them!"* (Numbers 11:29).

The Spirit's influence is claimed by many in the Old Testament; David claimed the Spirit spoke by him (2 Samuel 23:2) and Jesus substantiated this claim (Matthew 22:43). Many times in the New Testament we find where specific Old Testament prophecies are attributed to the power of the Holy Spirit (Acts 1:16; 28:25; Hebrews 10:15; et al).

Inspiration. The word "inspire" has many meanings today, but in the New Testament it has a singular meaning. The word is found in 2 Timothy 3:16: *"Every scripture inspired of God is also profitable for teaching, for reproof, for correction, for instruction which is in righteousness."* In the original Greek the word translated "inspiration" literally means "God-breathed." This clearly shows that the Scriptures are a divine product. This being true, Paul can appeal to the Scriptures as being accurate, reliable, relevant and useful. It is not the purpose of this work to prove the doctrine of inspiration but simply to see the Spirit's relation to this action of God.

The Spirit and Inspiration

What is the Spirit's exact relation to the inspiration of the word of God? This can be best seen from four lines of investigation: (1) The claim that Old Testament writers were spokesmen of the Holy Spirit of God; (2) The statements of the Saviour, apostles, and prophets in agreement with these claims; (3) The promise of divine guidance Jesus made to His apostles, in regard both to themselves and to their message; (4) The repeated claim of the apostles and prophets that they were speaking and writing the eternal truth of God through the Holy Spirit that had been given them.

The writers of the Old Testament assert, with little attempt to prove, that they were spokesmen on behalf of God by his Spirit. In a passage we have already noticed, David says, "*The Spirit of Jehovah spake by me, and His word was in my tongue*" (2 Samuel 23:2). In like manner Isaiah says, "*And as for me, this is my covenant with them, saith Jehovah: my Spirit that is upon thee, and my words which I have put in thy mouth, shall not depart out of thy mouth, nor out of the mouth of thy seed . . . saith Jehovah, from henceforth and forever*" (59:21). One of the most vivid claims along this line is found in Ezekiel 11:5: "*And the Spirit of Jehovah fell upon me and said unto me, Speak: Thus saith Jehovah.*"

These claims of the prophets find sufficient confirmation in the New Testament. Jesus Himself attributes to David's words the power of the Holy Spirit (Matthew 22:42-46; Mark 12:35-37; Psalms 110:1). In Acts 1:16 Peter says, "*The scripture should be fulfilled, which the Holy Spirit spake before by the mouth of David.*" In Acts 28:25 Paul applies a prophecy of Isaiah to a current situation: "*Well spake the Holy Spirit through Isaiah the prophet unto your fathers.*" Peter later tells us that, although these men were empowered to speak by the Holy Spirit, they did not always understand the full significance of what they spoke (1Peter 1:10-12).

It is the Spirit who was to teach the apostles (John 14:26) and to recall to their minds all that Jesus had taught them, thus leading them into all the truth (John 16:13). The Holy Spirit of God is to guarantee both the correctness of the witnesses and the trustworthiness of their message. This is especially seen in John 16:12-15:

> *I have yet many things to say unto you, but ye cannot bear them now. Howbeit when he, the Spirit of truth, is come, he shall guide you into all the truth; for he*

shall not speak from himself; but what things soever he shall hear, these shall he speak; and he shall declare unto you the things that are to come. He shall glorify me; for he shall take of mine, and shall declare it unto you. All things whatsoever the Father hath are mine: therefore said I, that he taketh of mine, and shall declare it unto you.

Notice the following facts from this passage: (1) Christ specifically states that even for His apostles he would leave many things unrevealed by his earthly life and teaching (v. 12); (2) Christ also gives them assurance that such revelation would come through the Holy Spirit (v. 13); (3) With such truth and guidance from the Holy Spirit the apostles would be spokesmen of Christ, speaking with all of His authority (13:20; 17:20).

Last of all, the apostles demonstrated in their writings that they firmly believed that their message was God's message through the Holy Spirit of God who had empowered them to so speak and write. Paul's claim for his message was that it was not the product of man's wisdom, nor was an understanding of it attainable by man's wisdom, but that his message was simply the revelation of God through the Spirit (1 Corinthians 2:6-13). He further claimed that God's entire purpose in Christ had thus, by the Spirit, been revealed to the apostles and prophets (Ephesians 3:5). Peter said the things that had been hinted at by prophets of old had now been openly preached unto us by men of the Spirit (1 Peter 1:10-12).

Because of these facts, we conclude in the same conviction with which we began this chapter: The Holy Spirit of God is the author of God's word of life.

Because the Holy Spirit both revealed the facts contained in Scripture and inspired the words in which they are written, because in every case of conversion we find that the word of

God was proclaimed, and because men were convicted thereby of their sins, many honest, sincere seekers of truth have reached the conclusion that the Spirit and the word are one and the same thing. Others, viewing these same scriptures, have reached the conclusion that the Spirit does nothing immediately, but that he does all things through the written word. We will now turn our attention to these two positions.

The Holy Spirit and the Word of God

That the word and the Holy Spirit of God are two different things is abundantly clear in manifold passages, many of which we have already noticed in this chapter. In 2 Samuel 23:2 David makes a clear distinction between the Spirit that spoke by him and the word that the Spirit spoke. In Ezekiel 2 the Spirit falls upon Ezekiel and he is told to speak the word of God. But, perhaps Ephesians 6:17 shows the separation between the Spirit and the Word better than any other passage: *"And take the helmet of salvation, and the sword of the Spirit, which is the word of God."* The Spirit and the word are no more the same than is the soldier and his sword. One is the weapon and the other is the power behind the weapon.

In Romans chapter eight we find a work that the Spirit "Himself" does – that of interceding on behalf of the saint's unutterable groanings:

> *And in like manner the Spirit also helpeth our infirmity; for we know not how to pray as we ought; but the Spirit himself maketh intercession for us with groanings which cannot be uttered; and he that searcheth the hearts knoweth what is the mind of the Spirit, because he maketh intercession for the saints according to the will of God* (Romans 8:26-27).

Here is a work of the Spirit separate from His work through the written word. We will discuss the intercession of the Holy Spirit of God in another chapter.

In Psalms 139:7-10 David attributes the work of providential leading to the Holy Spirit of God.

> *Whither shall I go from thy Spirit? Or whither shall I flee from thy presence? If I ascend up into heaven, thou art there: If I make my bed in Sheol, behold, thou art there. If I take the wings of the morning, And dwell in the uttermost parts of the sea; Even there shall thy hand lead me, And thy right hand shall hold me.*

Notice verse 10: *"Even there thy hand shall lead me, and thy right hand shall hold me."* In Acts 8, when the Lord wanted Phillip to go preach to the Eunuch, the Spirit led the preacher to the sinner. In Acts 16 the Spirit forbade Paul to preach in Asia and Bithynia and led him into Macedonia. Even so today God answers our prayers by leading us to where the lost are. The Holy Spirit of God has thus been active in our lives. The man who believes that God answers prayer must believe that the Holy Spirit works providentially.

SUMMARY

The Holy Spirit of God revealed the will of God, inspired the recording of that will, and today works through that will converting men to God and Christ. The Spirit aids the saint's prayers when moments of grief, anxiety, or joy make words impossible and leads the soul-winner to the lost by His providential care and oversight. These are the relations that the Spirit of God sustains to the Word of God.

QUESTIONS

Chapter Three

1. Since God wants man to know Him, He has revealed Himself in creation as well as in His inspired word. Discuss how the created world manifests God

2. What is the difference between "revelation" and "inspiration?" How do the work together?

3. What part does the Holy Spirit play in the revelation of God's will? Illustrate with Scripture and reasoning.

4. Since Jesus told His apostles in John 16:12-15 that they could not "bear" the many things He had to say to them; and since the Holy Spirit was to guide them into all (further) truth, might we expect the apostles to speak of some things which Jesus never spoke of in the Gospels?

5. Some teach that the Holy Spirit and the Word are one and the same. Show by Scripture and reasoning that this is not the case.

Chapter Four

THE HOLY SPIRIT OF GOD AND THE LIVING WORD

Introduction

The Holy Spirit of God is the author of life. He is the author of the Word of Life, which is the *"power of God unto salvation unto everyone who believes"* (Romans 1:16).

He who is called the Spirit of the Father is also termed the Spirit of Christ or the Spirit of Jesus. The Scriptures reveal an intimate relationship between the work of the Son and the Spirit. This association between the Son and the Spirit is revealed in much more detail than the relationship between the Spirit and the Father.

We might even entitle this section the Messianic Spirit. Not that the Spirit is our Redeemer, but Jesus could not have been our Redeemer except for the Holy Spirit of God. This will be the burden of our study in this chapter.

In order to appreciate more fully the activity of the Holy Spirit in the life of Christ, we need to see the uniqueness of the Son of God. He existed in perfect equality with the Father before becoming flesh (Philippians 2:5-6) and had done so from all eternity (John 1:1). He was, and is, God Himself (Hebrews 1:8): Holy, omniscient, omnipotent, omnipresent, eternal. When the fulness of time had come, He came to earth to take upon Himself human flesh (Galatians 4:4). Thus He became the only one who can rightfully be called both God and man. Never ceasing to be altogether God, He became altogether man.

This very fact, that Jesus is altogether God as well as man, has, more than likely, contributed more than anything else to a neglecting of, or at least of minimization of, the essential ministry of the Spirit in the life of Christ. The Bible plainly teaches that Christ was eternal (John 1:1); He likewise came into time (John 1:14). He was completely God (Philippians 2:5-6); He became completely man (Philippians 2:7-8). In the life and ministry of the one called Jesus Christ, from His incarnation to His complete glorification, the Holy Spirit of God is completely operative.

The Holy Spirit Prophesies the Coming of Christ

Centuries before the coming of Christ into the world the Spirit, through the prophets, had told in minute detail the birth, life, ministry, death and resurrection of Jesus. Following is a list of some of those prophecies:

Prophecies of Christ's Coming.

1. Seed of woman (Genesis 3:15).
2. Descendent of Shem (Genesis 9:26-27).
3. Seed of Abraham (Genesis 12:3; 18:18; 22:18).
4. Of the tribe of Judah (Genesis 49:10; Micah 5:2).
5. Of the stock of Jesse (Isaiah 11:1-2; 10).
6. Of the lineage of David (Isaiah 9:7; Jeremiah 23:5).

Prophecies of Christ's Birth.

1. Born of a virgin (Isaiah 7:14).
2. Born in Bethlehem (Micah 5:2).
3. Born while temple still stood (Malachi 3:1).

4. Flight into Egypt (Hosea 11:1).
5. Killing of the male children (Jeremiah 31:15).

Prophecies of Christ's Life and Ministry

1. A prophet like Moses (Deuteronomy 18:15-18).
2. A priest like Melchizedek (Psalms 110:4).
3. His ministry in Galilee (Isaiah 9:1, 2).

Prophecies of His Last Days.

1. His triumphant entry into Jerusalem (Isaiah 62:11; Zechariah 9:9).
2. His betrayal by a friend (Psalms 41:9).
3. Sold for 30 pieces of silver (Zechariah 11:12, 13).
4. Details of His trial and crucifixion.
    a. His silence when accused (Isaiah 53:7).
    b. His many sufferings (Isaiah 53:4-6).
    c. The piercing of His hands and feet (Psalms 22:16; Zechariah 12:10).
    d. The insults and mockings (Psalms 22:6-7; 109:25).
    e. Offered gall and vinegar (Psalms 69:21).
    f. Lots cast for His garments (Psalms 22:18).
    g. Not a bone to be broken (Psalms 34:20; John 19:36).
    h. His burial with the rich (Isaiah 53:9).
5. His resurrection (Psalms 16:10).
6. His ascension (Psalms 68:18; 110:1).

According to God, speaking through His servant Isaiah, the Messiah was to have the Spirit of Jehovah resting upon Him (11:2). These attributes of wisdom, understanding, counsel, might, knowledge, fear of Jehovah and judgement were deemed essential to the carrying out of the work of the Messiah and were to be His through the Spirit of Jehovah.

The function of the Spirit was also to be closely related to the ministry of the Messiah.

Behold, my servant whom I uphold; my chosen, in whom my soul delighteth: I have put my Spirit upon him; he will bring forth justice to the Gentiles. He will not cry, nor lift upon his voice, nor cause it to be heard in the street. A bruised reed will he not break, and a dimly burning wick will he not quench: He will bring forth justice in truth. He will not fail nor be discouraged, till he have set justice in the earth; and the isles (Gentiles) *shall wait for His law* (Isaiah 42:1-4).

Matthew states that the healing ministry of Jesus fulfilled this passage (12:15-21).

The full significance of all of this is seen in the numerous times the Holy Spirit is connected in Old Testament prophecy to the Messianic time, the Messianic purpose, and the Messianic kingdom (Isaiah 32:15-20; 44:3-5; Ezekiel 36:26-31; Zechariah 12:10). The wilderness of the hearts of men is to be changed into a fruitful field by the Spirit. The dry desert of human life is to be moistened by the gentle rain of the Spirit's influence. By the bestowal of the Spirit upon mankind, the rebellion of human nature is to be converted into humble, contrite obedience to divine law.

The Holy Spirit and The Incarnate Word

The doctrine of the Virgin Birth has been attacked consistently and constantly because of its central importance to the Christian faith.

The relationship of the Holy Spirit of God to the virgin birth of Christ is clearly set forth in the first chapter of both Matthew's and Luke's inspired gospel accounts. Gabriel's announcement to Mary is the most complete: *"The Holy Spirit shall come upon thee, and the power of the Most High shall overshadow thee: wherefore the holy thing which is begotten shall be called the Son of God"* (Luke 1:35).

Notice Matthew's simple statement: *"Now the birth of Jesus Christ was on this wise: When his mother Mary had been betrothed to Joseph, before they came together she was found with child of the Holy Spirit"* (Matthew 1:18). The angel appeared to Joseph and said, *"Fear not to take unto thee Mary thy wife: for that which is conceived in her is of the Holy Spirit"* (Matthew 1:20). The Holy Spirit of God thus enabled the Eternal Word to become the Incarnate Word. The power behind the virgin birth of Christ was the Holy Spirit of God.

In passing from this subject, notice some proofs presented for the virgin birth: (1) It was announced by the angel (Luke 1:35); (2) It occurred by the power of the Spirit (Matthew 1:18); (3) Instruction was given to Joseph (Matthew 1:20); (4) Jesus is born (Matthew 1:24-25; Luke 2:1-7).

The Spirit and the Ministering Word

The activity of the Holy Spirit in the personal ministry of Christ is even more evident than His part in the birth of Christ.

The Spirit is present and active in the baptism of Jesus. When Jesus came up out of the water, the Spirit descended upon Him in bodily form as a dove (Luke 3:21-22). The result of this is seen in Luke 4:1: *"And Jesus, full of the Holy Spirit, returned from the Jordan, and was led up in the Spirit in the wilderness during forty days, being tempted of the devil."* The imperfect tense is used in this verse to indicate the Spirit's continuing presence with Christ. This is also seen in Luke 4:14, after the completion of the temptation: *"And Jesus returned in the power of the Spirit into Galilee: and a fame went out concerning him throughout all the region round about."*

The influence of the Spirit upon Jesus can best be seen by a study of Luke 4:16-22. Jesus had spent nearly all of the first thirty years of His life in Nazareth. He had gone to Judea to be baptized of John. The Spirit had descended upon Him, led Him into the wilderness of temptation, preserved Him in his temptation. Now He is back home and will preach in the synagogue. About the time a Jewish boy reached the age of eighteen he began to read the Scriptures in the synagogue. So those Jews had heard Jesus read for approximately twelve years, but today there was going to be a difference.

> *And he came to Nazareth, where he had been brought up; and he entered, <u>as His custom was</u>, into the synagogue on the Sabbath day and stood up to read. And there was delivered unto him the book of the prophet Isaiah. And he opened the book and found the place where it was written, The Spirit of the Lord is upon me, because he anointed me to preach good tidings to the poor: he hath sent me to proclaim release to the captives, and recovering of sight to the blind, to set at liberty them that are bruised. To proclaim the acceptable year of the Lord. And he closed the book and gave it back to the attendant, and sat down: and the eyes of all in the synagogue were fastened on him. And he began to say unto them, "Today hath this scripture been fulfilled in your ears. And all bare him witness, and wondered at the words of grace which proceeded out of his mouth: and they said, Is not this Joseph's son?"* (Luke 4:16-22).

At least two things are of significance here; First, the statement that the Spirit has anointed Jesus and therefore Jesus is ready to enter His ministry; and second, that the Spirit has so made a difference in the life of Christ that these men now marvel at His teaching. Jesus would not have been able to amaze men with His teaching except for the Holy Spirit of God.

The work of the Spirit in the life of Christ can be seen in the miracles that Jesus wrought. In Matthew 12 Jesus drove a demon out of a blind and dumb man. The Pharisees said He had done it by Beelzebub the prince of demons. To which Jesus replied, *"If I by Beelzebub cast out demons, by whom do your sons cast them out? . . . But if I by the Spirit of God cast out demons, then is the kingdom of God upon you"* (Matthew 12:27-28). The significance of this is plain: Except for the Holy Spirit of God, Jesus would not have been able to perform the great miracles that He did.

This is not to depreciate the Deity of Christ, but is simply to state that as a man Jesus needed the power and influence of the Holy Spirit of God in His life. If He did, how much more do we?

The Spirit and The Crucified Word

The work of the Spirit in the life of Christ was a complete ministry. The Spirit also sustained Jesus in His sufferings. In one way the entire life of Christ was one of suffering, but in that last week of His life, the suffering reached its summit and climax in the cross. From what we have already studied, we would be ready to infer that the Spirit sustained Jesus in this great moment of trial. However, we are not dependent upon that inference, for the Scriptures clearly teach that the Spirit enabled Jesus to offer himself as a sinless sacrifice to God: *"How much more shall the blood of Christ, who through the eternal Spirit offered himself without blemish unto God, cleanse your conscience from dead works to serve the living God?*" (Hebrews 9:14).

The Spirit and the Resurrected Word

In Ephesians 1:19-20 Paul speaks of the great power God used in raising Christ from the dead. He says it is this same power that works in us. In John 10:17-18 Jesus claims the Father had given Him power to lay His life down and to take it up again. Thus both the Father and the Son had a part in the resurrection of Christ. Does the Holy Spirit stand in similar relationship?

First of all, from the nature of the case we would say He does. The Spirit had been the agent in bringing Christ into the world, empowering Him in His ministry, preserving Him in His temptations and enabling Him to die sinless. Could we then believe that He had nothing to do with Christ's resurrection? But we are not left to inference alone, for in Romans 8:11 Paul says, "*If the Spirit of Him that raised up Christ Jesus from the dead dwelleth in you, He that raised up Christ Jesus from the dead shall give life also to your mortal bodies through his Spirit that dwelleth in you.*" Paul says that God will give life to our mortal bodies in the same manner (seen by "also") as He did to Christ's, that is, through His Spirit. See also 1 Peter 3:18-21.

As Jesus would have not come from the virgin womb of Mary except for the Spirit of God, He would not have come from the virgin tomb of Joseph of Arimathea had it not been for the executor of the will of the Godhead, the Holy Spirit of God.

The Spirit and the Glorified Word

The glory that rightfully belongs to Christ is variously presented in the Sacred Record.

There is that glory that the Eternal Word had with the Father in eternity: "*And now, Father, glorify thou me with thine own self with the glory which I had with thee before the world was*" (John 17:5).

Then there was the glory that the cross brought Him. As He explained to the disciples on the way to Emmaus: "*Ought not the Christ to suffer these things and to enter into His glory?*" (Luke 24:26). In Philippians 2, Paul says that Jesus existed in the very form of God but emptied Himself and became a servant. Then he concludes, "*Wherefore God highly exalted him, and gave unto him the name which is above every name*" (v. 9).

Of those who belong to Him and the Father, Jesus affirmed, "*I pray for them: I pray not for the world, but for those whom thou hast given me; for they are thine; and all that are mine are thine, and thine are mine: and I am glorified in them*" (John 17:10). Hence, Jesus is glorified in his disciples.

It is in changing people in order that they might belong to Christ and the Father that the Spirit plays such a vital part. It is as Jesus said, "*He* (The Holy Spirit) *shall glorify me: for he shall take of mine, and shall declare it unto you*" (John 16:14).

In the eternal counsel of God it was through the Holy Spirit that His Son became a man, victoriously withstood all Satanic temptation, and was anointed for His threefold office of Prophet, Priest and King. As such He perfectly revealed the will of God and achieved the redemption of all mankind by His living, dying and rising again.

Even now, in the withdrawal of the visible presence of our Lord from us, the Holy Spirit of God is His personal representative, His Vicar, among us. The Holy Spirit of God is indeed the Spirit of Christ Jesus.

QUESTIONS

Chapter Four

1. What did the fact of the Spirit of Jehovah resting upon Him have to do with the earthly ministry of Jesus?

2. Discuss the part the Holy Spirit had in the virgin birth of the Messiah. How does the unbelieving world view this event?

3. What conclusion does Richard draw from Luke 4:16-22 and Matthew 12:27-28 concerning the influence of the Holy Spirit in the life of Jesus?

4. What part, if any, did the Holy Spirit play in the resurrection of Jesus from the dead?

5. Concerning the Holy Spirit and the glorified word, how does the Holy Spirit bring glory to the Son?

Chapter Five

THE HOLY SPIRIT OF GOD
AND THE CHURCH

Introduction

To find out the relationship that the Holy Spirit of God sustains to the church of God one must make a close and careful examination of the first two chapters of the book of Acts. It is here that the apostles became, by *the power* of the Holy Spirit, the guides and judges of the Israel of God. It is in these two chapters that we see the preparation for His coming and His actual coming.

The apostles received a commandment to wait (Luke 24:49; Acts 1:4-5). It is as if Jesus had said, "You cannot do my work without my Spirit."

The apostles received from Jesus a promise of power (Acts 1:8). When the Spirit promised in verses 4 and 5 comes upon them, He would give the power necessary to witness on behalf of Christ. The word for power is *dunamis,* which is the basis for our word "dynamite." Thus the Spirit was to supply the disciples with the dynamism necessary for the fulfilling of their task. The Apostles waited with prayer and supplication (1:14). They waited in the right place (the city of Jerusalem) (1:13).

They waited in fellowship (1:14). They waited in study of the Scriptures (1:16-20).

In prayer, in meditation on God's word, in uninterrupted fellowship, the disciples waited for the Spirit, and the Spirit came.

The Promise
"Ye Shall Be Baptized in the Holy Spirit"
(Acts 1:5b)

This promise of Jesus to the Apostles is one of the most controversial sayings ever to pass from the lips of our Saviour.

Those who take their theology from John Calvin naturally view this passage as a command to wait fatalistically for the Spirit to come and give the apostles "an experience of grace" that would testify to their hearts of their salvation. They feel that unless and until one has been baptized with the Holy Spirit he cannot begin to look in the direction of God for salvation.

The Pentecostal and Holiness people urge those whom they believe to be possessors of salvation to go on further and obtain the "baptism of the Holy Spirit" which will empower them to speak in tongues, prophesy and perform other things of miraculous nature.

The time-honored position among the brethren has been that this promise ("*Ye shall be baptized in the Holy Spirit*") was made to, and for, only the twelve apostles. That this is not true can be shown conclusively from the Scriptures. It is also contended that this was *a special measure* of the Holy Spirit given to guide the Apostles into all truth. That this too is incorrect we will see in this section.

What Baptism Is Not

Before we discuss what this promise is and means, let us clear some debris and see some things that it cannot be.

It is not anything administered by anyone other than Jesus

In Matthew 3:8-12; Luke 3:13-17 and John 1:31-34, John the Baptist declares that Jesus, and Jesus alone, would be the baptizer with the Spirit and fire. So when we find something that we think might be the "baptism" of the Spirit, if anyone other than Jesus is the baptizer, we know that we have the wrong thing.

It is not anything that took place before Pentecost

In Matthew3:11; Mark 1:8; Luke 3:16 and John 1:33, we read that Jesus is to baptize in the Holy Spirit. In John 7:39 we see that the Spirit is promised but not given because Jesus had not yet been glorified (Cf. Acts 2:33). Since we have already studied the fact that the Spirit was in existence and active in the Old Testament times, even in creation, we know that something new and unique concerning the Spirit is in view here. In Acts 1:4-5 the baptizing in the Spirit is still to take place in the future: "not many days hence."

It is not the power to perform miracles

This is evident since the Apostles had performed miracles before this promise was given in Acts 1:4-5 (Cf. Luke 10:17-20). In the Old Testament many of the mighty men of God were miracle workers (Elijah and Elisha in particular). If the apostles had already performed miracles before Acts 1:4-5, then the promise has nothing to do with the performing of miracles.

It is not inspiration

The apostles had spoken by inspiration before. This promise was made in Acts 1:4-5 (Matthew 10:19). Countless men and women had been inspired of God before Christ came to the earth. Men such as Isaiah, Ezekiel, Elijah, Daniel and other Old Testament prophets had been inspired of God. Therefore we can see the promise made by John the Baptist and endorsed by Jesus was not inspiration. If this promise was inspiration then evil men had already received it (compare the lying prophet in 1 Kings 13, Saul the son of Kish, and Caiphas).

It is not the power to speak in tongues

We know this mainly because this power is not given by Jesus but by the Spirit himself (1 Corinthians 12:11). Jesus gave the Spirit to these Gentile Corinthians when they became sons (Galatians 4:6; 3:14). The Spirit gave them power, miraculous and other-wise, as He willed. Also, before Pentecost Balaam's ass was empowered to speak with the tongue of man and no one believes he was baptized with the Spirit.

It is not to be filled with the Spirit

This is evident from the fact that men and women were filled with the Spirit before Pentecost and no one was baptized in the Spirit before Pentecost. In Luke 1:15 the promise is made that John the Baptist would be filled with the Spirit from his mother's womb. In Luke 1:41 John leaped within his mother's womb and Elizabeth was filled with the Spirit. In Luke 1:67 Zachariah, John's father, was filled with the Spirit and prophesied. So these three, John the Baptist, Elizabeth, and Zachariah, were filed with the Spirit and all before Pentecost. A study of Ephesians 1:13; 5:18-19 and Colossians 3:16 will reveal that to be filled with the Spirit means to be influenced by the Spirit through the revealed word taking up its permanent abode in our heart fully. Any influence from the Spirit, miraculous or otherwise, could not be the fulfillment of the promise, *"Ye shall be baptized in the Spirit."*

It is not a mere clothing with the Holy Spirit

There are those who believe this to be the best phrase to use in regard to this promise of Jesus. Luke 24:49 speaks of the Apostles being "clothed with power from on high." It is assumed that the "clothing" is by the Holy Spirit (i.e. that He is the garment) despite the fact that it plainly states that they will be "clothed with *power.* " The person who can see no difference between the Spirit Himself and the power given by the Spirit cannot discern between the Spirit and the Word.

Consider also that many men were clothed with the Holy Spirit in the Old Testament (Judges 6:34 mg ASV; 2 Chronicles 24:20 mg; 1 Chronicles 12:18 mg). Think this over! Men during the Mosaic era were "clothed" with the Holy Spirit, yet they had not the "baptism" of the Holy Spirit. Therefore, this promise is not merely a clothing with the Holy Spirit.

It was not to make one a son of God

The Calvinists teach that one must be baptized with the Holy Spirit in order to become a son of God. In this connection they quote 1 Corinthians 12:13. Not knowing the scriptures, they apply a passage that talks of baptism in water to the baptizing in the Spirit. That this passage (1 Corinthians 12:13) relates to water baptism is evident from just a few considerations:

1.   Galatians 4:6 tells us God gives us the Holy Spirit *because* we are sons. That there is no time element between our becoming sons and the reception of the Spirit is of no consequence. This only shows God's promptness to give what He promises. In the plan and mind of God we become sons and then He gives us the Spirit.

2.   The Holy Spirit is the earnest of our inheritance (Ephesians 1:14) but only sons can inherit the Father's possessions. Therefore, only sons can receive the Spirit.

3.   Peter makes it clear in Acts 2:38 that the receiving of the Holy Spirit does not precede remission of sins, that it is an additional promise when obedience is rendered unto remission of sins.

When an elder is appointed by a congregation who submits to the stipulations laid down by the Spirit of God, he is said to be ordained by the Holy Spirit. The elders at Ephesus were doubtless selected by Paul and the local congregation, and yet he addressed them as men made overseers by the Holy Spirit (Acts 20:28).

> *Therefore take heed to yourselves, and to all the flock in which the Holy Spirit has made you overseers, to feed the church of God which He has purchased with His own blood.*

In John 4:1-2 we are told that Jesus made and baptized more disciples than John, although Jesus did not personally baptize any of them. If Jesus did not Himself baptize people, yet it is said of Him that he baptized because the apostles did it at His bidding, should we think it strange language for Paul to say the same thing about the Spirit? As Jesus baptized when the Apostles baptized, the Spirit baptizes as we baptize.

It is not a measure of the Holy Spirit

One passage is quite sufficient to destroy this theory forever. In John 3:30ff we read of Jesus and his testimony. The whole section deals with Jesus' authority to speak. The American Standard Version should be followed in this section. In the 34th verse, the King James is very wrong and seldom is more so. The passage should read, *"For he whom God hath sent speaketh the words of God: for he giveth not the Spirit by measure."*

This passage does not say the Father gives the Spirit, but that Jesus gives the Spirit without measure. Not too many believed the testimony of Jesus, but John the Apostle, writing many years after the glorification of Jesus, claims the giving of the Spirit by Jesus to be one of the proofs of His claim to be God's own Son and Prophet. (See John 7:38 and Acts 2:33.)

This passage categorically states that Jesus does not give the Spirit by measure. This buries forever "the measure theory." Furthermore, how could one have a "measure" of the Spirit when the Spirit is a person? Either we have the Spirit or we do not. (See Appendix on John 3:30-36.)

The reply normally will be, "I really mean a measure of His power or influence." Well, let us say what we mean. If we use unscriptural terminology, we will usually end up with unscriptural thought. Let us determine when the scriptures speak of the Spirit as God's gift to man and when it speaks of the gifts of the Spirit.

But granting that the King James was correct in its version of John 3:34, what would it prove? The words "unto him" are added to the text. If we left them out, it would leave the passage: *"For he whom God hath sent speaketh the words of God: for God giveth not the Spirit by measure."*

There are those who believe since the Scripture speaks of God giving Christ the Spirit without measure, it is necessarily implied that others receive the Spirit by measure. This does not necessarily follow. James said, *"Is any cheerful, let him sing psalms"* (5:13 KJV). Does this infer that the merry cannot pray or sing spiritual songs? Of course it does not. Neither does John 3:34 infer a measure theory, even from the King James Version.

The Wording of the Promise

Read carefully Matthew 3:1-12; Mark 1:1-8; Luke 3:1-9, 15-17; John 1:32-34; Luke 24:49; Acts 1:4-5, 8; 2:1-4, 14-21, 33, 38-39.

The thesis of this author, based on the preceding verses, is that the statement *"Ye shall be baptized with the Holy Spirit"* is simply the promise of the outpouring of the Spirit by Jesus on the day of Pentecost one time for all, henceforth, available for all men whom God calls (through the gospel, 2 Thessalonians

2:14). The Spirit then empowered whom He willed to the degree He willed (1 Corinthians 12:4-11). To establish this we must examine the pertinent passages.

John the Baptist speaks to a mixed multitude of people. Some he had baptized; some he had refused to baptize. In Matthew 3:11 he declares,

> *I indeed baptize you with water unto repentance: But he that cometh after me is mightier than I, whose shoes I am not worthy to bear: he shall baptize you with the Holy Spirit and with fire.*

This passage makes it clear that Jesus would baptize more than twelve men with the Holy Spirit, unless we are to take a very singular view of it indeed. Luke 3:15-16 tells us the words which John spake were addressed to all the multitude.

> *The **people** were waiting expectantly and were **all** wondering in their hearts if John might possibly be the Christ. John answered them **all**, "I baptize **you** with water. But one more powerful than I will come, the thongs of whose sandals I am not worthy to untie. He will baptize **you** with the Holy Spirit and with fire."*

It must be obvious that John led these people to believe they (i.e. those whom he baptized) would be baptized in the Holy Spirit. To make the first "you" different from the last "you" is without warrant by hermeneutics.

John came preaching repentance (Matthew 3:1-2). However, the condition of the people to his preaching called forth a two-fold thrust to his message: Baptism for the remission of sins for the repentant, Mark 1:4; Luke 3:3; 7:33; and judgement (or wrath) to come for the unrepentant, Matthew 3:7 (Cf. Malachi 3:1-6; 4:1-6; Luke 1:17). So John tells the

Jews in Matthew 3, and the parallel passages, that after him was coming the Saviour and Judge of the world, the One who would pour forth on the whole Jewish nation God's Spirit and God's fire of judgement.

In Matthew 3:10 John the baptist mentions an axe which was *already* laid at the root of a tree. There can be no doubt but that he had reference to the beginning of the end of Judaism, which end came at the hands of the conquering Titus. In the same verse he makes an allusion to a fire which is certainly not intended to be taken literally. As a figure, it is literal fire, but with a figurative application. In verse 11 he mentions the "baptism of fire" and in verse 12 he mentions fire again, and here it is obviously a judgement, but which judgement?

We need to remember that these words were spoken to a Jewish audience without any explanation. So, let us look to the Old Testament for our explanation. In Malachi 3:1-6 we read of Christ acting with fire among the Jewish nation as a refiner of silver and that a messenger would announce His coming. The dross will be burnt off and the pure silver will remain. In Malachi 4:1 we notice Christ acting with fire as a burner of stubble. In 4:2 He heals the righteous. In Malachi 4:5-6 the "day" which accords with the day of 3:2 and 4:1 is described. Elijah (John the baptist, Matthew 11:14; Mark 9:11-13; Luke 1:17) will come preaching reformation before the "*great and terrible day of Jehovah come*" (Malachi 4:5-6). This is manifestly the same judgement of which John speaks in Matthew 3. "Fire" in verse 10 is the completion of a judgement already begun or ready to be accomplished. "Fire" in verse 12 refers to the destruction of the Jewish unbelievers, which was promised by the prophet Malachi. Therefore "fire" in verse 11 would refer to the same thing. There is little doubt but that this was the judgement of which John spoke and this was the judgement upon hardened Israel, the destruction of Jerusalem by Titus in 70 A.D.

The unprofitable Jewish chaff was burnt up with *unquenchable fire* when Jerusalem was destroyed in 70 A.D.

The unfruitful Jewish trees were cut down and thrown into the fire when Jerusalem was destroyed in 70 A.D.

Therefore, the unfruitful, unprofitable Jewish nation was baptized in fire when Jerusalem was destroyed in 70 A.D. (See appendix on "Fire Passages.")

Hence, the baptism of fire referred to an event, the outpouring of judgement upon the entire nation. This would make sensible an analogous situation in regards to the baptizing in the Spirit (i.e., that it would refer to an event to take place sometime in the history of Israel to the fruitful and profitable among the nation.)

Now let us notice the passages in the first two chapters of the book of Acts (1:4-5, 8; 2:1-4; 14-21, 33, 38-39). Jesus states that the apostles were to receive what the Father had promised and what He had told them about (cf. John 14-16) when they were baptized with the Holy Spirit not many days from his ascension. In verse eight an additional promise is given: Power, after the Holy Spirit came upon them. Notice carefully the order in verse 8: first, the Holy Spirit was to come upon them, and second, they were to receive power. Compare John 14:26 and 16:13. These passages state that Jesus and the Father will send the Spirit, and the Spirit will then empower the apostles. The Spirit is the power-giver not the power, per se. Both the power-giver and the power came in Acts 2:1-4. The Spirit fell on each of the apostles (they received the power-giver) and, then, the Spirit empowered them to speak in languages they had never learned.

The crowd that was gathered by the sound of a mighty wind marveled because of the manifest proof of God's power in the apostles. Some, however, mocked saying they were filled with new wine. Peter, on the contrary, taught that this was the result of the fulfilling of God's promise in Joel 2:28-32 that the Spirit would be poured out upon all of God's people, and that the power-giver would empower many more than just the apostles, even the Jew's sons, daughters, servants, and handmaidens, and king. In presenting proof of Jesus' resurrection, Peter cites scripture, the apostle's eye-witness, and concludes by pointing to the marvelous outpouring of the Spirit by Jesus as proof positive of his exaltation (cf. John 3:34; 7:38-39). Many of the Jews are convinced by Peter's reasoning and cry out to know what they must do. They are told to repent (change their mind completely concerning sin and God) and to be baptized (immersed). They are promised two blessings contingent upon this obedience: remission of sins and the Holy Spirit as a gift. Peter concludes this promised Spirit, now poured out by Jesus, is not only for the Jews at Pentecost, but for their children (all Jews that will ever live) and all that are afar off (the Gentiles, Ephesians 2:11-13), even as many as the Lord our God shall call unto Him. (That would be you and me if we are called by the gospel, 2 Thessalonians 2:14.) Three thousand accepted his words and were baptized, and according to Acts 5:32, God gave unto them what He had already given the apostles, the Holy Spirit.

We can easily see from Acts chapters one and two that the baptizing in the Spirit and the outpouring of the Spirit are just different ways to refer to the same event. Notice the following syllogisms.

The apostles were to receive from the Father the "baptizing in the Spirit" (Acts 1:4-5). The apostles received upon awaiting from the Father the "outpouring of the Spirit" (Acts 2:16ff).

Therefore, the "baptizing in the Spirit" was the "outpouring of the Spirit."

The promise of the Father was the "baptizing in the Spirit" (Acts 1:4-5).

The promise of the Father was "poured forth" by Jesus (Acts 2:33).

Therefore the "baptizing in the Spirit" was poured forth. This does not make pouring and baptism synonymous words. Pouring is the event from Jesus' viewpoint. Baptizing is the event from the recipient's viewpoint. A coin placed in a glass is immersed after water is poured upon it. The pouring is not the immersion. It is the water leaving the source. The immersion is not the pouring. It is the result, the covering of the coin. So it is here in this case.

John said, *"He will baptize you in the Holy Spirit"* (Matthew 3:7-12).

Jesus however, poured the Holy Spirit upon them (Acts 2:33).

Therefore, He baptized them when He poured the Spirit upon them. (The baptizing and the outpouring refer to the same event.)

It is now an easy task to prove that the "baptizing" or "outpouring" was a one-time, never-to-be-repeated act.

First of all, the word translated "pour forth" means "to pour out, to shed as blood, to gush out, to spill, to rush headlong into anything, be abandoned to." It is used in every case in the New Testament to mean pour forth all of whatever is being poured out. (See Appendix on "pour forth.") For some examples see the following from W. E. Vine's Expository *Dictionary of New Testament Words*, Page 196:

> "To pour out is used of (a) Christ's act as to the changers' money, John 2:15; (b) of the Holy Spirit, Acts 2:17, 18, 33; Titus 3:6; (c) of the emptying of the contents of the bowls (A.V. vials) of divine wrath, Revelation 16:1-4, 8, 10, 12, 17; (d) of the shedding of the blood of the saints by the foes of God, Revelation 16:6."

In all of these, an unlimited outpouring of all of the contents is in view. So in Acts 2 the word used indicates that all of the Spirit had been poured out for all men (2:17).

Then the tense of the verb "pour out or forth" indicates that it was to be a one-time-for-all-time operation. In Acts 2:17, when Peter quotes Joel's prediction concerning what will happen, the future tense is used. However, notice that Peter says what was promised has occurred: *"This is that . . ."* In verse 33 Peter says, *"He* (Jesus) *hath poured forth . . ."* Here Peter used the Aorist tense, which expresses action as a point completed in the past. So Jesus, according to Peter, had at one point in the past poured out the Spirit. Then in Acts 10:45, at the house of Cornelius, the writer, Luke, records the attitude of the Jewish Christians who had come with Peter: *"And they of the circumcision that believed were amazed, as many as came with Peter, because that on the Gentiles also was poured out the gift of the Holy Spirit."* The words "was poured out" express the perfect tense in the original language. (The Analytical Greek Lexicon, Page 124.) The perfect tense indicates an action completed in the past but resulting in a continuing and perfect state of being. The emphasis is on the completed state of being. (Essentials of New Testament Greek, Ray Summers, Page 103.) So, the Holy Spirit had in the past been poured out for the Gentiles (Acts 2:17, 39) and was still present and available for them upon obedience (Acts 5:32; Galatians 4:6). This was proved by the tongue-speaking occurring (v. 46, Cf. 1 Corinthians 14:22). Notice, (1) Joel spoke of it as *future,* but Peter says it *happened* on Pentecost (Acts 2:17); (2) Peter spoke of it as a *completed act in one point of time in the past* (Acts 2:33); (3) Luke spoke of it as a *completed act in the past but resulting in a continuing state of being* (Acts 10:45). Really, in the sermon on Pentecost, Peter stressed all three of these points, concluding that the Spirit was henceforth available for all whom God called (Acts 2:38-39).

From the preceding arguments from plain scripture we can draw only one conclusion: The event we call the *"baptism of the Spirit"* took place in Jerusalem. It happened once for all time.

In 1 Timothy 2:6 we read that Christ died a ransom for all. In like manner, in Hebrews 2:9, we find it was the Father's will that Christ die for all men. Christ did not die for an elect few but for every man who will ever live. However, only those who obey Him will benefit from this once-for-all death. Even so, on the day of Pentecost the Spirit was poured out for all men. However, only those whom the Lord *"our God shall call . . ."* (Acts 21:39) and those who call on God will partake of that once-for-all outpoured Spirit (Acts 2:21).

Some Objections Considered

Objection: In Acts 1:4-5 and John 14-17 the promise of the Holy Spirit was given to the apostles and to the apostles alone. Therefore, we are wrong in enlarging the promise.

It is quite true that the immediate hearers of the above verses are the apostles, but this does not necessarily limit the promise to them any more than the books of Corinthians, Thessalonians and Philippians are limited to those to whom they are addressed. If we desire to know how an evangelist is to conduct himself today, we read the letters written to Timothy or Titus.

The above objection is successful only if all the other verses on the subject limit it to the twelve, but this is not the case. Luke 3:15-17 cannot be so understood as to apply only to the twelve. If only the twelve (eleven at the time of Acts 1:4-5 and John 14-17) were promised the gift, then Matthias, Paul, and the household of Cornelius did not receive it, and Joel did not promise it to all flesh. Imagine Jesus seeking to limit the promise to twelve when He had already inspired Joel to promise it to all flesh!

Objection: If all men received the baptism of the Spirit, they would be able to work miracles and speak by inspiration.

This objection betrays a complete misunderstanding of the promise. The **giving of the Spirit** and the **imparting of power** are two entirely different actions. The Spirit is given **by** Jesus, but gifts and powers are given **by** the Spirit (1 Corinthians 12:11; John 16:13). *To confuse the power given by the Spirit and the Spirit himself is to miss the whole point.*

But it is objected that the baptism of the Spirit "invariably" brought power. This is simply begging the question.

The truth of the matter is, Christ poured out the Spirit for all men and gave the Spirit to all Christians. The Spirit, then, gave power to as many of them as he saw fit. To the apostles He gave so much, to others so much, and to us (no miraculous) so much (Ephesians 3:16). We, today, do not need miraculous power; therefore, He does not give it to us. Again let us keep a clear distinction between the Spirit as a gift and gifts from the Spirit.

Objection: If all Christians receive this baptism of the Holy Spirit, there are two baptisms, and Paul claimed there was only one.

The phrase *"baptized in the Holy Spirit"* spoke of an event and not a "measure" of the Holy Spirit. The careful student will have noticed that the expression *"baptism OF the Holy Spirit"* does not occur in the scriptures. Now, although this does not make it wrong (i.e., because it is not mentioned), its use immediately conveys a "measure" idea. Notice the different thoughts which creep into their usage:

Ye shall receive the "baptism of the Holy Spirit."

Ye shall be "baptized with the Holy Spirit."

In the first, they were to *receive* something to possess it. In the latter something was to *happen to* them. One does not receive a verb; it happens to him. (Read this over again and think about it, because it is important and will not register at first.)

What does all of this mean? We ought to avoid these phrases which confuse and can be easily misunderstood. John 3:34 is an inspired commentary on *"baptized with the Holy Spirit."* It makes it clear that the Spirit is given *without measure.* The word "pour" from Joel and from Acts 2:17 has the same idea of super-abundance. Jesus was indicating to what extent the Holy Spirit would be given when he said *"Ye shall be baptized . . ."*

To consider this promise (the baptizing) as a mere *clothing* with the Holy Spirit is to miss the whole point since many had before that day of Pentecost been "clothed" with the Holy Spirit. (See previous study) The emphasis is not on the baptizing but on the Spirit Himself.

> *When God gave the Spirit, He gave him without measure, He baptized the recipients with him, He poured him out for all flesh. This He did once for all time. Since Pentecost the Spirit has been available for all men.*

Whenever a person becomes a Christian he benefits from that initial outpouring, just as surely as did the apostles.

But more, when Joel spake of God pouring out His Spirit upon "all flesh," he did not have reference to "all nations." It had its application to his own people, even though Peter at the Spirit's leading extends the promise to all who obey. In the Old Testament only a few chosen men and women had any direct dealing with the Holy Spirit. Men like David, Samson, Gideon, etc., had experienced the workings and directing of the Spirit. But, Joel says, *"a day is coming when the Spirit will be poured out upon all flesh,"* not only certain chosen ones but handmaidens, servants, old men as well as young. Read Joel 2, beginning at verse 18 through the end of the chapter, and you will see that this promise is to the remnant of His people. Furthermore, in the era of the Messiah, the Spirit will come and live within the subject of the Christ. In this we find a second "new" aspect of the working of the Spirit in the Messianic Age.

Also when Paul wrote Ephesians chapter four the "baptism of fire" was still to come upon the Jewish nation and he was to undergo a "baptism of suffering."

Objection: The promise of Joel was not the "baptism" of the Spirit; this was something that Christ promised.

Christ said: *"Ye shall be baptized with the Holy Spirit"* (Acts 1:4-5)

Peter said: *"This is that spoken by the prophet Joel"* (Acts 2:16-17)

Jesus said the promise of the Father was the baptizing in the Spirit. Peter said that the Father had promised in Joel the outpouring of the Spirit. Therefore, the baptizing of the Spirit Jesus promised, is the outpouring of the Spirit Joel promised.

The activity of the Holy Spirit in the household of Cornelius presents problems to the Calvinist, the Pentecostals, and to people who believe the "measure" theory. An honest and open examination of this incident is absolutely necessary to our study. Read carefully Acts 10:1-11:18. Before discussing this complex question (for Calvinists, and many members of the church) let us establish some things from this section of scripture.

Major premise: Peter was to speak words whereby Cornelius was to be saved (Acts 11:14).

Minor premise: Peter was to speak all things commanded by God (Acts 10:33).

Conclusion: The words whereby he must be saved included all things commanded of God.

Major premise: Peter commanded him to be baptized in the name of the Lord (Acts 10:48).

Minor premise: The words whereby he was to be saved included all things commanded of God by Peter.

Conclusion: Baptism in the name of the Lord was included in the words whereby he would be saved.

The relation of Cornelius' baptism to his salvation can be seen by comparison.

Major premise: Peter preached only one gospel (Acts 15:9, 11).

Minor premise: In preaching the gospel in Acts 2 he commanded people (Jews) to be baptized (Acts 2:38).

Conclusion: In preaching the gospel to Cornelius (Gentiles), he would command baptism.

Major premise: Peter commanded people to be baptized in the name of the Lord "*unto the remission of sins*" (Acts 2:38).

Minor premise: Peter commanded Cornelius to be baptized in the name of the Lord (Acts 10:48).

Conclusion: Peter commanded Cornelius to be baptized for the remission of sins.

Whatever the people in Acts 2:38 were baptized "unto," Cornelius was baptized "unto." If they were baptized "because of" the remission of sins, then Cornelius was baptized "because

of" remission of sins. If they were baptized "unto" or in order
to the remission of sins, then Cornelius was baptized "unto" or
in order to the remission of sins.

Major premise: Whatever Peter told the people in Acts
                   2 to be baptized "unto" he also told
                   them to repent "unto."

Minor premise: Peter did not tell them to repent "unto"
                   (because of) the remission of sins.

Conclusion: He did not tell them to be baptized
                   "unto" (because of) the remission of
                   sins.

Major premise: He told them to repent "unto" (in order
                   to) the remission of their sins.

Minor premise: He told them to be baptized for the
                   same reason he told them to repent.

Conclusion: He told them to be baptized "unto" (in
                   order to) the remission of sins.

Major premise: Peter told the people in Acts 2 to be
                   baptized unto the remission of sins.

Minor premise: Peter preached but one gospel (Acts
                   15:9, 11).

Conclusion: He told Cornelius to be baptized "unto"
                   (in order to) the remission of sins.

Briefly reconstructing what occurred at the house of
Cornelius we have: An angel appears to this devout man, tells
him his prayer is heard, to send to Joppa and fetch Peter, who
would tell him words whereby he would be saved. Peter comes
and as he begins to preach (Acts 11:15), the Spirit falls upon
Cornelius and the other Gentiles present. Peter then commands
them to be baptized in the name of the Lord. Peter returns to
Jerusalem and rehearses to the brethren the conversion of the

Gentiles. The brethren rejoice that God has granted the Gentiles repentance unto life also (Acts 10:1-11:18).

The problems that normally come to mind in this section are "When was Cornelius saved?" and "Did he actually receive the Spirit (to indwell) before he was baptized?" This second question is sometimes phrased, "Was Cornelius baptized in the Holy Spirit?"

The answer to the first question is simple. Cornelius was saved when his sins were removed. His sins were removed when he was baptized (refer to the discussion just completed). So he was saved when he was baptized, not before he was baptized. This will help us to answer the second question when we come to it.

In preparation of the answer of the second question: "Did Cornelius receive the Spirit before baptism? Was he baptized in the Holy Spirit?" we need to consider the purpose of this miracle of the Spirit coming upon him.

The purpose of something can normally be seen in the use made of it, and this would always be the case with inspired men. What use or uses did Peter make of the coming of the Spirit upon Cornelius and the other Gentiles? Only one use was ever made of this occurrence: To break down the prejudice of the Jews, to enable them to see that the Gentiles could be baptized (become Christians) without being circumcised (becoming a Jew). In Acts 10:47 Peter asked if the Jews present could forbid the Gentiles from being baptized, seeing they had received the Spirit? In Acts 11:16-17, when speaking to the brethren in Jerusalem, Peter again mentions the incident and the brethren rejoice in the Gentiles' salvation. Then, in Acts 15, when the brethren take the problem of circumcision to the apostles, Peter refers to this incident for the third time in an appeal to the Jewish Christians not to bind circumcision on the Gentile Christians. Since this is the uniform usage made of the incident, we would have to say, "The Spirit came upon Cornelius before he was baptized to prove once and for all that which Peter had stated in Acts 2:21 and 39 – that all, both Jew and Gentile, could be baptized, have their sins remitted, and receive the Holy Spirit." Peter did not regard this miracle as an end in itself, but simply used it as a proof that these men could be baptized.

In Acts 11:17 Peter speaks of "withstanding God." What did Peter mean by these words?

1.   Did he mean he could not withstand God in visiting the man's house? No! He was already in the man's house when the Spirit fell.

2.   Did he mean it would be withstanding God not to preach the gospel to the man? Certainly not! He had already begun to do this when the Spirit fell.

3.   Was it in acknowledging that all men are acceptable to God? No! This he had confessed before the Spirit fell.

4.   What is the only thing he said after the Spirit fell? *"Can any forbid the water, that these should not be baptized, who have received the Spirit as well as we? And he commanded them to be baptized in the name of Jesus Christ"* (Acts 10:47-48).

From all of this we learn that to have refused to baptize these Gentiles in the name of the Lord would have been to withstand God.

But withstand God in what? What had God in mind for these men? That they might be saved! And we have already concluded, from the Scriptures, that the words whereby Cornelius and his house were to be saved included all that God had commanded through Peter. So Peter, in order not to withstand God, commands them to be baptized in the name of the Lord in order that God might have His way in this man's life. But God's purpose in this man's life was that he might be saved (Acts 11:14). Therefore, God through Peter commanded them to be baptized.

An objection would understandably be raised right here. "If Cornelius received the Spirit before baptism, he must have been saved before baptism!" Despite the cries of some who believe the "measure" theory, this objection is valid if Cornelius received the Spirit. It makes no difference "why" he received the Spirit. If he received the Spirit, the following is true:

1.   He was sealed unto salvation before he was baptized (Ephesians 1:13).

2.   He had the earnest (guarantee) of his inheritance before baptism (Ephesians 1:14).

3.   He was a son before he was baptized (Galatians 4:6).

4.   He was in God and God was in him before he was baptized (1 John 3:24; 4:13).

That these four things were not true can be seen in the study of the following plain passages – Acts 2:38; Galatians 3:27-28; Mark 16:15-16; Titus 3:4-6; et al.

The answer to this objection can be easily seen when we understand Luke's use of a certain figure of speech. The words in the Bible are to be understood in their literal meaning unless doing so would involve an absurdity or a contradiction of other plain passages. If we understand the words which describe Cornelius receiving the Spirit before baptism literally, we are left with four apparent contradictions of other plain passages, as we noted above. These words, then, must be understood to be some figure of speech.

The figure of speech Luke used here seems to be his favorite. A quick count of the book of Acts will reveal over twenty occasions of its use. It is called a metonymy. Webster's definition of a metonymy: "Use of one word for another that it suggests, as the effect for the cause, the cause for the effect, the sign for the thing signified, the container for the thing contained," etc.

Let's notice a few examples of this figure of speech. In Acts 6:7 we read of the word of God increasing. This does not mean that they added some to the word of God, but that the effects or results increased. In Acts 8:28 we find that the eunuch "read the prophet Isaiah." Here the prophet is named when his writings are meant. In Acts 8:14 we read that "Samaria had received the word." Here the city is named when the people are meant. In Acts 21:21 Paul is accused of teaching the Jews "to forsake Moses." Here Moses is named when the law is meant. In Acts 27:29 we read *"And fearing lest haply we should be cast ashore on rocky ground, they let go four anchors from the stern, and wished for the day."* Here the people are named when the ship is meant.

In Acts 2:33 we find Peter naming the gifts of the Spirit when he means the Spirit himself: *"Being therefore at the right hand of God exalted, and having received from the Father the promise of the Holy Spirit, he hath poured forth, this which ye see and hear."*

Everyone knows the Spirit is invisible. What these Jews saw was the apostles speaking in languages they ought not to have known. But what they saw and heard was NOT what Jesus poured forth. He poured forth the Holy Spirit, the promise of the Father, and yet Peter told them Jesus poured forth WHAT THEY SAW AND HEARD! Here the gifts are named when the Spirit is meant.

In Acts 8:12-20 the Holy Spirit is expressly named four times when the "gifts" are meant. Every Bible student is aware that those who obey the gospel, and are thus made sons, automatically receive the Spirit (Acts 2:38-39; 5:32; 2 Corinthians 1:21-22; Galatians 4:6). These people had heard the gospel (Acts 8:5-6); they had believed the gospel (Acts 8:12); they had obeyed the gospel, being baptized (Acts 8:12). They had, therefore, received the Holy Spirit. Yet Peter and John came down from Jerusalem that the Samaritans might receive the Holy Spirit (Acts 8:15). After the apostles had prayed and laid their hands on them, the record says, *"and they received the Holy Spirit"* (Acts 8:17). The key to the whole section is verse 18: *"Now when Simon saw that through the laying on of the apostles' hands the Holy Spirit was given, he offered them money."* We can see from this and the former consideration of the Spirit coming to all obedient believers, that this is a metonymy. The Spirit is stated when the gifts are meant.

In Acts 19:2-6 the Spirit is named when the gifts are meant. Paul approaches these whom he believes to be Christians (believers) and asks, *"Did ye receive the Holy Spirit when ye believed?"* (Acts 19:2). A very singular question to ask of those whom you believe to be Christians! Unless he meant, "Have you received any gifts of the Spirit since ye believed?" Verse 6 shows this to really be the question Paul was asking: *"And when Paul had laid his hands upon them, the Holy Spirit came upon them; and they spake with tongues and prophesied."* The Spirit is named when the gifts are meant. Also when Paul asked this question, they replied, *"Nay, we did not so much as hear whether the Holy Spirit was given."* Paul then asked them concerning their baptism, knowing that this was where believers are given the Spirit by God (Acts 2:38-39).

In Acts 4:8 we read of Peter being *"filled with the Holy Spirit."* In Acts 4:31 the same thing is said of a whole company of Christians. This was a qualification of the first deacons in Acts 6, and characterized both Paul and those whom he converted to Christ (Acts 13:9, 52). On these occasions, and all others where this expression is found, a metonymy is being employed. Here the power or influence is meant and not the Spirit himself. If a man receives the Spirit he has all that can be received. BUT THERE IS A WORLD OF DIFFERENCE BETWEEN OUR HAVING ALL OF THE SPIRIT OR THE SPIRIT HAVING ALL OF US!!!

If a man is not filled by the person of the Spirit which dwells within when he first believes, he never can be, for the Spirit Himself does not grow in size or magnitude. However, His influence and power in our lives and in the lives of the early Christians does and did grow.

So here in Acts 10:47, where it states that Cornelius' household received the Holy Spirit, it means that they received from the Spirit a gift, specifically the gift to speak in tongues (Cf. 1 Corinthians 12:11). This is exactly what Peter referred to in Acts 11:15-16 when he said that the Gentiles received the "like" gift as the apostles did "at the beginning." Let those who believe in the "measure" theory contend with this passage. The word translated "like" means "equal, in quality or quantity." It is translated "equal" five times. If the "measure" theory is correct, and Cornelius received the "baptism of the Spirit," then he became what the apostles were. The "like" gift (equal in quantity or quality) which Cornelius received was the speaking in tongues (Acts 10:44-46), the exact same gift that the apostles received "at the beginning" (Acts 2:1-4). So, again, the Holy Spirit is named when the gifts are really meant.

Someone might make one parting objection: "But it says the 'gift of the Spirit' was poured out upon Cornelius and his whole household." This is made to mean by the objector that these Gentiles received the Spirit as a gift from God before they were baptized. The difficulty of this verse (Acts 10:45) is removed immediately by a shallow study of the original language. The verse reads, *"And they of the circumcision that believed were amazed, as many as came with Peter, because that on the Gentiles also was poured out the gift of the Holy Spirit."* The verb translated "was poured out" is the perfect tense. This tense indicates an action that has been completed but which has also resulted in a continuing and perfect state of being. So this verse really serves as the Spirit's commentary of Acts 2:17-18, 33, 38-39. The Spirit on the day of Pentecost had been completely poured out for the Gentile as well as the Jew. This had resulted in a state of His being available for all whom God calls (Acts 2:39; 2 Thessalonians 2:14). The Gentiles this day were to receive what God had poured out for them in the past. The tongue-speaking was God's sign to the Jews, who did not believe that the Gentiles could be saved apart from circumcision, that the Gentiles were acceptable to God through obedience to the gospel without any recourse to the Law of Moses, and therefore could receive the Spirit without receiving Moses. 1 Corinthians 14:22 states that tongues are a sign to those who believe not, and these Jews did not believe that the Gentiles could be baptized without being circumcised.

CONCLUSION

So what happened at the house of Cornelius? The first uncircumcised Gentiles became Christians through the preaching of the gospel and their obedience to the same. They received from the Spirit the gift of speaking in tongues, as a sign to the Jews, before they were baptized. Then, they received from God what he had already provided for them at Pentecost, the Holy Spirit as a gift. Even Peter had not understood the full significance of the outpouring at Pentecost until God empowered these Gentiles. (Acts 11:15-16 states that this incident "reminded" him of Jesus' promise.)

QUESTIONS

Chapter Five

1. List and discuss individually several things which the "baptizing in the Holy Spirit" is not and cannot be.

2. Being "filled with" or "full of" the Holy Spirit is a popular concept today. Discuss what it means to "be filled with the Holy Spirit" and how Christians today are filled with the Spirit.

3. Discuss the Calvinistic view of being baptized in the Holy Spirit and why this view cannot be true.

4. Why do some people hold to the teaching that the Holy Spirit is given by measure? Is this biblically true? Explain why or why not.

5. Discuss what is meant by the phrase, "ye shall be baptized in (or with) the Holy Spirit and who this promise is spoken to.

6.	To what did John have reference when he spoke of being "baptized with fire" and the "axe laid at te root of the tree?"

7.	Does the "baptizing in the Holy Spirit" and the "pouring forth" of the Holy Spirit refer to the same event? If so, explain how.

8.	Explain how we can be sure that the baptizing in the Holy Spirit was a one-time for all-time occurrence.

9.	How can we know whether the promise of the Holy Spirit was for all believers or only for the apostles?

10.	If the promise was to all believers, why should not all believes be gifted to perform miracles?

11.	When was the Holy Spirit given to Cornelius to indwell and when to empower him?

12.	In what way would Peter have "withstood" God had he refused to baptize Cornelius?

13.	Name and discuss four things which would be true if Cornelius received the Holy Spirit before he was baptized.

THE TEMPORARY MIRACULOUS GIFTS FROM THE SPIRIT

Introduction

The references to miraculous gifts are not too numerous but are sufficient to show the existence of them in the apostolic days, their purpose, how they were conferred and that they were to cease with the confirmation of the Spirit-revealed word.

Before discussing the various individual passages dealing with miracles, let us remind ourselves that there is a clear and definite distinction to be made between the Holy Spirit as a gift and the gifts from the Holy Spirit. Christ is the giver of the Spirit–to the apostles and to all who obey (John 7:38-39; 14:16-17; Acts 2:38-39; 5:32; Galatians 3:14; 4:6). The Spirit gave miraculous power as He willed (1 Corinthians 12:4-11, esp. v. 11).

That the early church was supplied with miraculous gifts from the Spirit is evident from such passages as Romans 12:6-8; 1 Corinthians 12-14; Acts 8:14-18 and others. In the first two of these references some gifts are mentioned which are not at all miraculous; for example, in Romans 12:8 we read of the gift of "giving." This is a very needed gift today. When we finish this discussion on miraculous gifts from the Holy Spirit of God, we will discuss these non-miraculous, permanent graces.

A period of miracles is always a time when special testimony is needed to the authority of God's messengers.

There are three notable times in history when miracles were prominent: (1) The period of Moses, when they witnessed to his office as prophet and leader, causing the people to accept his message as from God; (2) the period of Elijah and Elisha, when apostasy made necessary an unusual witness to the power of God to call a people out of idolatry back to Himself, especially since there were no priests true to God; and (3) the period of Christ and the apostles. In the time of Christ, miracles were needed to witness to His person, to give proper credentials for the Messiah, and, in the case of the apostles, to demonstrate that their gospel was a message from God.

✳   With the completion of the New Testament, and its almost universal acceptance by those true to God, the need for further display of miraculous works ceased. Today there is no need for preachers to back up what they say by an appeal to the miraculous. John 20:30-31 teaches that the recorded miracles are sufficient to accomplish what the actual performance of miracles did. It is evident that those today who are claiming these temporary gifts have shown a gross indifference to the Bible. Some have stated in public, "I don't care what the Bible says; God speaks to my heart." The history of these sects is most convincing testimony that the undue seeking of miraculous powers often results only in excesses of the most *unholy* kind. Now let us look to the temporary, provincial, miraculous graces distributed by the Spirit in apostolic times, using 1 Corinthians 12, Romans 12, and Ephesians 4 as our guide.

APOSTLESHIP. The word apostle means a delegate, messenger or one sent with orders (Thayer, p. 68). There are apostles of Christ, empowered by Him to speak for Him, and apostles of the churches empowered by them for some specific task. The qualifications of the apostles of Christ Jesus are as follows: (1) They were chosen by the Lord Himself (Matthew

10:1-2; Mark 3:13-14; Luke 6:13; Acts 9:6, 15; Galatians 1:1). (2) They were supplied with miraculous powers which were to serve as credentials for their office (2 Corinthians 12:12; Acts 1:6; 2:43; 5:12; 16:16-18; 28:3, 9). (3) The indispensable qualification was that they should be eyewitnesses of the resurrected Lord (Acts 1:22; 2 Corinthians 9:1). (4) Their function was to lay the foundation of Jesus (1 Corinthians 3:11) and be the judges of the church (Matthew 19:28). Apostles are distinguished from prophets, teachers, and workers of miracles, etc. (1 Corinthians 12:28). The apostles had also the prophetic gift and worked miracles (2 Corinthians 12:12), but not all who had these two gifts were apostles. The apostolic office died with the first generation of Christians, there being no provision for successors. The fact that apostles were chosen from those who were eyewitnesses of Jesus' glory eliminates the possibility of later generations participating in the call of apostleship.

PROPHECY. Second only in importance to the apostles were the prophets. This gift was evidently possessed by many in apostolic days. Agabus predicted a famine in Acts 11:27-28 and Paul's imprisonment and sufferings in Acts 21:10-11. Barnabas, Simeon, Lucius, Manaen and Paul are mentioned among the prophets and teachers at Antioch (Acts 13:1). The four virgin daughters of Philip possessed the gift of prophecy (Acts 21:9), indicating that in the New Testament, as in the Old, this gift was not limited by sex. Judas and Silas, as prophets of God, were sent along with the prophetic letter in Acts 15:32. In all probability all the apostles possessed the gift of prophecy.

A contrast might aptly be drawn between the Old Testament prophets and the New Testament prophets. Both were God's special spokesmen; both gave warning that sin unrepented of brought judgment; both were aware that their message was God's, not theirs; both dealt with present problems as well as told of future promises. The main difference lay in the fact that the Old Testament prophet was a national leader, reformer and often patriot, delivering his message to the nation. The New Testament prophet's message was individual and personal; it revealed the will of God which otherwise would have remained unknown. This function was later filled by the revealed and written word of the apostles and prophets, the New Testament.

What were the qualities of the New Testament prophet? (1) He received God's message by some form of special revelation (Ephesians 3:5); (2) He was given divine guidance in declaring this message, corresponding to the inspiration of the written word; (3) He had to bear the stamp of divine approval and authority. The prophet, if a true prophet, must deliver a message free from error, a product not of his own mind, but a revelation of God's mind. The importance of the prophetic gift is declared in 1 Corinthians 14, where it is set forth as the greatest of gifts. This was because it dealt with edifying, exhorting and comforting the church (1 Corinthians 14:3). Probably related to the prophetic gift is the "word of wisdom" and the "word of knowledge" given to some by the Spirit (1 Corinthians 12:28).

While there are teachers, exhorters and evangelists today it is a safe conclusion that there are no longer any prophets. With the completed New Testament there is no further need for additional revelation. Paul told Timothy, before the completion of the New Testament, that he should teach what he had learned from Paul (2 Timothy 2:2). This is also sufficient for us today. The solemn warning of Revelation 22:18-19, the last to be written of the New Testament, is that God's judgment will rest upon those who add to the book, a reference specifically to the book of Revelation, but embodying a principle which underlies the whole canon (Jude 3).

MIRACLES. This is the first in the list of lesser gifts. The use of "then" *(epeita)* in 1 Corinthians 12:28 makes it clear that the order is deliberate. First things are being put first. The word for miracles is *dunameis,* meaning inherent power, power residing in a thing by virtue of its nature (Thayer, p. 159). In 2 Corinthians 12:12 it is grouped with signs, wonders and mighty works as the proof of an apostle. Miracles were, therefore, a display of divine power with a view of authenticating the apostolic or prophetic gift. Therefore, when the men these miracles witnessed to no longer existed, the power to perform these miracles ceased.

HEALING. This is a specific aspect of the gift of miracles. Miracles might pertain to matters of judgment (Acts 13:11), but healing always pertained to the restoring of health to the body, or mind, or both. While the gift of healing is no longer bestowed, God is able to, and does, heal in answer to prayer and faith. No one today, however filled with faith and powerful in prayer, is able to heal in virtue of an abiding gift.

TONGUES. There is more controversy over this one gift than over the rest of them combined. A complete and thorough refutation of the modern heresies surrounding tongue-speaking would be the occasion of another volume at least the size of this one; and, God willing, the author plans such a book in the very near future. (Richard died before he could write this book.) In this present study we will content our self with the study of the problem, the nature of the gift, the temporary nature of the gift, and a comparison of the glossolalia of the New Testament and that of today's Pentecostalism.

The place to start is Acts chapter two. Here is the first instance in all the history of the world of men receiving from the Spirit of God the power to speak in languages they had never studied. This phenomenon amazed unbelievers who came to the scene. They readily admitted that they all heard in their own language (Acts 2:8-11) the wonderful works of God being extolled. In Acts 10:46, in connection with the conversion of Cornelius and his household, a second instance of speaking in tongues is seen. The formal extending of salvation to the Gentiles was attended by this miracle, linking it to Pentecost. Peter refers to this in Acts 11:15-17. A third occasion of tongue speaking is Acts 19:1-6. Paul had discovered some disciples of John the Baptist who had never heard the gospel of grace and, accordingly, had not turned in faith to Christ. Following their baptism, Paul laid his hands upon them and the Spirit empowered them to speak in tongues and prophesy. In these passages from Acts there is no explanation at all concerning the purpose of this gift. This will be discussed in the only other passage in the New Testament that mentions "tongues" (1 Corinthians 12-14).

In 1 Corinthians 12:28, in a list clearly arranged in order of importance, speaking in tongues is mentioned last. Then in 1 Corinthians 13 it is stated to be useless unless accompanied by love (v. 1) and temporary, (v. 8). The entire fourteenth chapter deals more or less with the problem of tongues and prophecy in the church at Corinth.

In chapter 14 several very important points relating to tongue-speaking are made.

1.   He who speaks in a tongue speaks in the direction of or unto God and not unto man (v. 2).

2.   Tongues are inferior to prophecy as a means of edification, exhortation and comfort (vs. 3-4). Five words with

understanding are better than ten thousand words in a tongue (v. 19).

3.   Paul lists three actions that are engaged in by these who speak in tongues – praying, singing, and giving of thanks. Notice that all of these are directed toward God (vs. 14-17, cf. v. 2).

4.   Tongues should not be used in the assembly unless an interpreter is present (vs. 26-28).

5.   Tongues are a sign to the unbelievers and not intended for the edification of believers (vs. 21-22).

Four very important lines of argument prove conclusively that speaking in tongues was a temporary gift:

First, it is obvious that speaking in tongues began on Pentecost. It was not a part of God's gifts in the Old Testament era nor during the personal ministry of Christ; therefore, it must be of peculiar and special function, as we have already seen.

Second, speaking in tongues was in no sense a test of salvation. Since it was but one of the gifts of the Spirit, it is clear that not all Christians possessed it even in apostolic times. If tongues were essential, even as an outward sign of salvation, it is inconceivable that it should not be given a prominent place in the recording of the plan of salvation.

Third, the gift of speaking in tongues was no sure indication of great spirituality. Corinth, of all the churches Paul wrote, manifested the most carnality and open sin, yet speaking in tongues was more in evidence there than in the other churches. It is a matter of record that those who believe in tongues today have not led the way in holiness of living, but rather have been guilty of all manner of excesses.

Fourth, speaking in tongues is listed by Paul with prophesy and miraculous knowledge as being "in part" and to cease (1Corinthians 13:8-10). The temporary nature of these miraculous gifts is contrasted in this section with the permanent nature of **faith**, **hope**, and **love**, especially **love**.

It is a strange thing, but just a shallow comparison of the modern glossolalia with the New Testament phenomena of tongues will reveal that they are in no way similar.

1.   Paul declares in the matter of prophecy and tongue-speaking that women are to be silent (1 Corinthians 14:34).

2.   Paul says tongue-speaking was not for edification of others (1 Corinthians 14:4). Pentecostalism states that tongues are for the edification of all men.

3.   Paul says the gift of tongues was given for the benefit of the unbeliever (1 Corinthians 14:21-22).

4.   The Bible teaches that the tongues were real, actual languages (Acts 2:1-8). Pentecostalism teaches that they are ecstatic, unintelligible sounds, the meaning of which is known only to God.

From this it is easy to see that whatever is going on among these modern tongue-speaking groups, it is in no way related to the tongues mentioned in the New Testament.

INTERPRETING TONGUES. The gift of interpreting tongues (1 Corinthians 13:10; 14:26-28) was simply the divinely-wrought ability to translate the speech of those speaking in tongues. Since speaking in tongues is no longer existent in the church today, it is clear that the gift of interpreting tongues has likewise passed from the present purpose of God.

DISCERNING SPIRITS. Wherever there is the true, you will find the counterfeit. The devil would incite men to imitate what the Spirit was inspiring men to do in the gifts we have already studied. There was the need of somehow being able to distinguish between what was Spirit-inspired and what was devil-incited. The gift of discerning spirits (1 Corinthians 12:10) was the ability given by the Holy Spirit to discern the true from the false sources of supernatural revelation given in oral form. As the New Testament was completed, this gift would cease to have any reason for existing. Christians are dependent now upon the written Word of God as revealed by the Holy Spirit of God, and no one is given authority to discern spirits apart from that belonging to all Christians alike.

The New Testament demonstrates in several different ways the fact that these miraculous gifts were to cease in just a few years from the time that the Word was being recorded by the apostles and prophets. First of all, the way in which these gifts were conferred prove them to be temporary. Notice Acts 8:5-25. Here Philip, a man full of the Spirit (Acts 6:3) and able to perform great signs and miracles (Acts 8:13) which amazed the Samaritans (and Simon the sorcerer in particular), was unable to impart this gift to others. Neither did God give them any miraculous power directly from heaven. But, when word reached Jerusalem of Samaria's conversion, two of the apostles, Peter and John, were sent in order that the Spirit could fall upon these disciples and empower them miraculously. After they had prayed, they lay their hands on the Samaritans, and the Samaritans then manifested some power from the Spirit that Simon the Sorcerer, a man whose heart was not right (Acts 8:21), who was in the gall of bitterness and in the bond of iniquity (Acts 8:23), could see immediately (Acts 8:18). What they received through the laying on of apostolic hands was something appealing to a man who was used to having people recognize in him great power (Acts 8:9). The only conclusion that can be reached is that the Samaritans had received from the Spirit (1 Corinthians 12:11), through the disposition of the apostles' hands, some miraculous powers. In Acts 19:1-6 the Ephesians are likewise empowered, and in 2 Timothy 1:6 Timothy is reminded of the gift (perhaps prophecy) that is in him by the means of Paul's hands. 1 Timothy 4:14 teaches that the elders had agreed with this gift because they had laid their hands on Timothy at the same time, probably committing him to the work of being Paul's fellow-laborer. (Cf. Acts 13:1-3 and 14:26.) So we see that these miraculous gifts were only bestowed through the laying on of apostolic hands. If gifts were to continue, then apostles must continue to live to lay on hands, but when James was beheaded no one was chosen to take his place. Miracle-working therefore ceased with the death of the last man upon whom the apostles had laid their hands.

Then, the New Testament plainly states that miraculous spiritual gifts were temporary as compared to the non-miraculous graces. In 1 Corinthians 13 Paul contrasts the *termination of* miraculous gifts with the *continuance* of faith, hope and love. Notice verses 8 through 13:

> *Love never faileth: but whether there be prophecies, they shall be done away; whether there be tongues, they shall cease; whether there be knowledge it shall be done away. When I was a child, I spake as a child, I felt as a child, I thought as a child; now that I am become a man, I have put away childish things. For now we see in a mirror, darkly; but then face to face: now I know in part; but then shall I know fully even as also I was fully known. But now abideth faith, hope, love, these three; and the greatest of these is love.*

Then the biblical purposes of miracles also demonstrates their temporary, provisional character. The miracles of Christ were, according to the biblical account for two purposes: (1)

They were to incite and cause within man belief in Jesus that he was indeed the spokesman of God (John 10:32-38) and, (2) they were to strengthen and deepen the faith of His disciples (John 11:11-16). John 20:30-31 shows that the written record of these miracles is sufficient today to accomplish both of these purposes: *"Many other signs therefore did Jesus in the presence of the disciples, which are not written in this book; but these are written, that ye may believe that Jesus is the Christ, the Son of God; and that believing ye may have life in His name."* John states that when we read his record of some of the signs that Jesus performed, we may have both saving belief and life eternal in Jesus' name. This settles once for all any claim that miracles need to be performed today to cause men to believe. If man will not believe on examining the word of God, he will not believe if he could see a repetition of every single miracle that Jesus performed. The word of God is sufficient to belief and eternal life.

The miracles of the apostolic era are seen to have a three-fold purpose. **First**, as we mentioned in this treatise, they served as credentials for the apostles, proving that they were from God and spoke with His authority and in His stead (2 Corinthians 12:12; Acts 2:43; 5:12; 2 Corinthians 5:18-21). The twelve would have forever been dismissed as ignorant Galileans by their Jewish contemporaries if it had not been for their power to perform miracles (Acts 2:5-12, 43; 3:1-11; 4:13-14, 21-22, 29-33; 5:12-24; et al). And Paul would have never been accepted, even by the churches that he established, as an apostle equal to the twelve without the same miraculous power (2 Corinthians 12:12; Romans 15:18-19). Since this work was done for the original apostles, and since they have no successors, there is no longer any need for miracles to establish the authenticity of any apostolic office.

A second purpose of the miraculous element in the apostolic church was to provide the means for finite men to become the tools through which the message of Christ Jesus could be trustworthily and unerringly delivered to men. Even in the Old Testament this was necessary as seen in 2 Peter 1:21: *"For no prophecy ever came by the will of man: but men spake from God, being moved by the Holy Spirit."* Also notice 1 Peter 1:10-11:

> *Concerning which salvation the prophets sought and searched diligently, who prophesied of the grace that should come unto you: searching what time or manner of time the Spirit of Christ, which was in them did point unto, when it testified beforehand the sufferings of Christ, and the glories that should follow them.*

The word "moved" in 2 Peter 1:21 means to be picked up and carried along by, as a ship is carried along by the wind. So the power that enabled prophets of old to speak was God's Spirit. In the second passage, 1 Peter 1:11, Peter attributes the words themselves to Christ's Spirit in the prophets. As in the Old Testament, so in the New; in 1 Corinthians 2:6-13 Paul states the power that made the apostolic message trustworthy and unerring:

> *We speak wisdom, however, among them that are full-grown: yet a wisdom not of this world, nor of the rulers of this world, who are coming to naught: but we speak God's wisdom in a mystery, even the wisdom that hath been hidden, which God foreordained before the worlds unto our glory; which none of the rulers of this world hath known; for had they known it, they would not have crucified the Lord of glory: but as it is written, Things which eye saw not, and ear heard not, And which entered not into the*

heart of man, whatsoever things God prepared for
them that love him. But unto us God revealed them
through the Spirit; for the Spirit searcheth all things,
yea, the deep things of God. For who among you
knoweth the things of a man, save the spirit of the
man, which is in him? Even so the things of God none
knoweth, save the Spirit of God. But we received, not
the spirit of the world, but the Spirit which is from
God; that we might know the things that were freely
given to us of God. Which things also we speak, not in
words which man's wisdom teacheth, but which the
Spirit teacheth; combining spiritual things with
spiritual words.

In this passage Paul claims that the Spirit of God had
taught him by revelation the things he knew about Christ Jesus.
(Compare Galatians 1:11-12.) He also states that when he was
ready to communicate it to man, he was not left to his own
wisdom or the wisdom of others for the way or the words, but,
that the Spirit, by inspiration, also provided the very words in
which to inerrantly convey the message of Christ. Thus, Paul
learned his message from the Spirit directly and received the
power to deliver his message from the Spirit directly. Indeed
the word of God is the sword that the Spirit has fashioned and
uses in the conversion of men today, and nothing more is
needed and nothing less will suffice. The apostles delivered the
message of the Spirit to the saints, the trustees of the message
(1 Timothy 3:15) one time for all time (Jude 3).

A third purpose of miracles in the first century was to
confirm the word that had been spoken by the apostles and
prophets through the power of the Holy Spirit of God. Two
passages are sufficient to indicate this purpose:

And he said unto them (the apostles, RR), *Go ye into*
all the world, and preach the gospel to the whole

creation. He that believeth and is baptized shall be saved; but he that disbelieveth shall be condemned. And these signs shall accompany them that believe: in my name shall they cast out demons; they shall speak with new tongues; they shall take up serpents, and if they drink any deadly thing, it shall in no wise hurt them; they shall lay hands on the sick, and they shall recover. So then the Lord Jesus, after he had spoken unto them, was received up into heaven, and sat down at the right hand of God. And they went forth, and preached everywhere, the Lord working with them and confirming the word by the signs that followed. Amen (Mark 16:15-20).

Hebrews 2:1-4 speaks in a very similar way:

Therefore we ought to give the more earnest heed to things that were heard, lest haply we drift away from them. For if the word spoken through angels (the Law of Moses, RR) *proved steadfast, and every transgression and disobedience received a just recompense of reward; how shall we escape, if we neglect so great a salvation which having at the first been spoken through the Lord, was confirmed unto us by them that heard; God also bearing witness with them, both by signs and wonders, and by manifold powers, and by gifts of the Holy Spirit, according to His will.*

Both of these passages state that Jesus, or God had confirmed or borne witness to the message of Christ as delivered in the speeches and writings of the apostles and prophets. It was therefore authoritative and divinely powerful to the saving of the souls of all men who would come in belief to Christ.

The word, according to the passages just noticed, was preached and confirmed. In Galatians 3:15 Paul states that confirmation is a final and unalterable act: *"Brethren, I speak after the manner of men: Though it be but a man's covenant, yet when it hath been confirmed, no one maketh it void, or addeth thereto."*

Notice also Hebrews 6:13-18:

> *For when God made promise to Abraham, since he could swear by none greater, he sware by himself, saying, Surely blessing I will bless thee, and multiplying I will multiply thee. And thus having patiently endured, he obtained the promise. For men swear by the greater: and in every dispute of theirs the oath is final for confirmation. Wherein God, being minded to show more abundantly unto the heirs of the promise* (these are New Testament Christians, Galatians 3:26-29) *the immutability of his counsel, interposed with an oath; that by two immutable things* (God's word and His oath, RR), *in which it is impossible for God to lie, we have fled for refuge to lay hold of the hope set before us.*

These passages show, beyond any argument, that confirmation is a one-time, final, unalterable and availing act. Since the word of God has been preached (1 Peter 1:20-12), confirmed (Mark 16:19-20; Hebrews 2:1-4), and delivered to the saints (Jude 3), there is no longer any need for the confirming miracles.

Miracles, then, were to cause belief, which the word of God now accomplishes (John 20:30-31; Romans 10:17); to deepen belief to total commitment, which the word of God now accomplishes (2 Peter 1:3-4; 3:18; Romans 1:16-17); to serve as credentials for the apostles, which they did and we have the written record; to cause the message to be trustworthily and inerrantly delivered to mankind, which purpose was accomplished (1 Corinthians 2:6-13; 14:37; 2 Peter 1:3-4; 1 Peter 5:12; Ephesians 3:3-5); and to confirm the word that was spoken and written, which they did once for all (Mark 16:19-20; Hebrews 2:1-4; Galatians 3:15; Hebrews 6:16). There is not today one single biblical purpose for miracles to exist.

One might make a parting objection: "But Jesus performed many miracles for a *benevolent* purpose. Miracles were also for the alleviating of man's sufferings." First of all, if this be so, then Jesus is to be criticized for not healing all of men's diseases. In Mark 7 Jesus told the Syrophoenician woman that he was not going to heal her daughter. Why? Did Jesus not love the Phoenicians? Of course, He loved all men. He told her His work pertained only to the House of Israel. In Mark 1:38-39 you can find that Jesus' primary mission was to preach, and that even His miracle-working was secondary to His preaching. Notice the passage: "*And he saith unto them, Let us go elsewhere* (all Capernaum was seeking him for healing, verses 32-37) *into the next towns, that I may preach there also; for to this end came I forth. And he went into their synagogues throughout all Galilee, preaching and casting out demons.*" So the miracles of Jesus were not for benevolent purposes but for evangelistic purposes, as He Himself declares in John 10:37-38 and 11:14-15 and as John, the writer declares in John 20:30-31. The recorded and confirmed word of God today is sufficient in and of itself and needs nothing to support it, but only someone to proclaim it.

QUESTIONS

Chapter Six

1. There were three distinct periods in history when miracles were prominent. Name these and discuss why this was so.

2. Since the gift of speaking in tongues was manifested in the early church, should it not be available today? Explain why or why not.

3. Signs and wonders, according to John 20:30-31, were powerful in convincing people in the time of the apostles that Jesus was the Son of God. Are they as powerful to accomplish the same thing today? Explain how.

4. What was the three-fold purpose of miracles in the early beginning of the church?

5. Some might say that Jesus performed "some" of His miracles for benevolent purposes. Is this true? If so, what would it say about Jesus' attitude toward all the hurting people He did not heal?

NON-MIRACULOUS PERMANENT SPIRITUAL GIFTS

Not all the spiritual gifts bestowed upon children of God are miraculous and temporary in their nature. For instance, in the lists given in the New Testament we have the following: (1) the gift of teaching, (2) the gift of helping or ministering, (3) the gift of administration or ruling or pastoring, (4) the gift of evangelism, (5) the gift of exhortation, (6) the gift of giving, (7) the gift of showing mercy, and (8) the gift of faith.

TEACHING. This gift is specifically named in Romans 12:7; 1 Corinthians 12:28; and in Ephesians 4:11. By the very nature of the case it must be considered as one of the major, and most desirable, gifts in the church today. It would seem from several considerations that this gift was mainly the ability to take newborn children of God on unto perfection. The teacher must understand the truth and be able to impart it. What will be required to obtain this gift? Paul gives Timothy the answer in 2 Timothy 2:2: *"And the things which thou hast heard from me among many witnesses, the same commit thou to faithful men, who shall be able to teach others also."* All that is required, as far as personal power is concerned, is for the individual to be faithful to God. All that is needed, as far as power is concerned, will be supplied by learning the Word of God. Faithful men are made by God to be able men through the Word of God. Preachers, are you fulfilling 2 Timothy 2:2 in training teachers? Fellow Christians, are we fulfilling 2

Timothy 2:2 by presenting ourselves for training in God's Word?

MINISTERING OR HELPING. It is impossible to conceive of a Christian that does not have the ability to help in some way. However, in Romans 12:7 and 1 Corinthians 12:28 we see some are given special ability along this line. Paul is not talking about natural abilities but spiritual gifts. Deacons, women-helpers and all other servants who have the special knack of relieving one's burdens or work-load would be included in this gift. The distinctions within the gift are many, different individuals being able to minister in different ways, thereby retaining a peculiar quality to the gift according to the purpose of God in its bestowal. The apostles would have been hindered in their work of praying and preaching if men had not possessed this gift (Acts 6:1-6). Because seven such men could be found we read, "*And the word of God increased; and the number of disciples multiplied in Jerusalem exceedingly; and a great company of the priests were obedient to the faith*" (Acts 6:7). God give us more helpers like these! God help me to be a helper like these!

ADMINISTRATION, RULING, OR PASTORING. 1 Corinthians 12:28 lists governments or administrations. Thayer defines the word as "a governing, a government, wise counsels" (page 364). It is used in the Septuagint, (a Greek translation of the Old Testament), in Proverbs 11:14: "*Where no wise guidance is, the people falleth; But in the multitude of counselors there is safety.*" A different word from the same root word is used in Acts 27:11 and Revelation 18:17. Thayer defines this word, "steersman, helmsman, sailing-master" (Page 364). The men possessing this gift would be, then, those responsible for guiding the church's and the Christian's barge through the difficult straits of life – the elders. (Compare Hebrews 13:17).

Romans 12:8 lists "ruling" as one of the graces that God had supplied the church in Rome. Thayer defines this word, "1. in the trans. tenses *to set or place before; to set over* (no New Testament usage, RR). 2. in the pf. plpf. add 2 aor. act. and in the pres. (as it is in our text, RR) and impf. mid. a. *to be over, to superintend, preside over,* A.V. rule), 1 Tim. v. 17; with a gen. of the pers. or thing over which one presides, 1 Th. v. 12; 1 Tim. iii. 4 sq. 12. b. To be a protector or guardian; to give aid ... Rom. 12:8. c. To care for, give attention to: Titus 3:8, 14." (Page 539-These are all of its usages in the New Testament.) Again we can see the gift here in view is that of being made capable of being an elder, a ruler, of God's church.

In Ephesians 4:11 one of the gifts God gave the church for its perfection was that of "pastor." Thayer defines this word, *"a herdsman, esp. a shepherd,* a. prop. Matt. 9:36; 25:32; 26:31; Mk. 6:34; 14:27; Lk. 2:8, 15, 18, 20; John. 10:2, 12; 10:11, 14. b. metaph. *the presiding officer, manager, director, of any assembly:* so of Christ the Head of the Church, John 10:16; 1 Pet. 2:25; Heb. 13:20, of the overseers of the Christian assemblies, Eph. 4:11" (page 527). Again the gift here in view is the furnishing of men, elders, who will guide, protect, nourish, and, if necessary lay down their life for the sheep, the church of God.

So even elders have nothing to boast of except that the Holy Spirit has given them the gift of governing, guiding and shepherding God's people. *"What hast thou that thou didst not receive? but if thou didst receive it, why dost thou glory as if thou hadst not received it?"* (1 Corinthians 4:7).

EVANGELISM. This gift, mentioned in Ephesians 4:11, has primary reference to preaching the gospel to the unsaved in an effort to bring them to Christ. Thayer defines the word, *"a bringer of good tidings, an evangelist."* This name is given in the New Testament to those heralds of salvation through Christ who are not apostles: Acts 21:8; Eph. 4:11; 2 Tim. 4:5" (page 257–the only three times word used in New Testament). While it is the sovereign duty of all Christians to tell others about Christ (Revelation 12:11), there are those men who are given the special gift of being able to move effectively the hearts of multitudes to come in obedience to the gospel of Christ Jesus. One with the gift of evangelism may also possess other spiritual graces, such as teaching, exhorting, showing mercy, etc. However, his primary responsibility is to fulfill his primary ability at every opportunity. *"But be thou sober in all things, suffer hardship, do the work of an evangelist, fulfill thy ministry"* (2 Timothy 4:5).

EXHORTATION. This grace, listed in Romans 12:8, is a very practical gift, being primarily an appeal to action. Thayer defines the word, "a calling near, imploration, supplication, entreaty, exhortation, admonition, encouragement, consolation, comfort, solace, univ. persuasive discourse, stirring address,– instructive, admonitory, consolatory, powerful ... discourse." God give us more men who can stir us to action.

GIVING. It seems strange at first to find "giving" listed with the graces, or gifts, God bestows upon the church in Romans 12:8. But a moment's reflection gives many clues why this was necessary. While everyone has the gift to give to some degree, not everyone has the ability to do so with singleness of heart. (Notice the marginal reading in the American Standard Version.) And, when we consider what kind of giver God is pleased with, we come to realize the necessity of God's help in the matter. God is only pleased with the giver who does so (1) regularly or habitually (1 Corinthians 16:2), (2) as he has been prospered (1 Corinthians 16:2), (3) abundantly (2 Corinthians 8:7), (4) willingly–with singleness of mind (2 Corinthians 8:11-12), (5) as an expression of his love (2 Corinthians 8:24), (6) according to purpose or forethought (2 Corinthians 9:7), (7) in faith, trusting God for the needs of life (2 Corinthians 9:8-11; compare Matthew 6:22 and Luke 6:38), and, perhaps the most difficult of all, (8) cheerfully (Gr. *hilaros*) (2 Corinthians 9:7). It would appear as if the true test of the grace of God is the matter of giving. May God give to each one of us the grace to be a regular, proportionate, abundant, willing, loving, purposeful, trusting, cheerful giver! May God cause each one of us to understand that, "*it is more blessed to give than to receive*" (Acts 20:35).

SHOWING MERCY. This is the concluding grace or gift that Paul says God had bestowed upon the church at Rome. All of us have known those Christians who can walk into a hospital room or some other place of need, and radiate love and cheerfulness to everyone there. When they left we felt like we had truly been benefitted by their being there. This gift would seem to fall mostly in the realm of giving succor to those who were sick, afflicted. All of us can show mercy to a certain degree, but the one with this gift can do so with cheerfulness. May God grant unto us more radiant, happy dispensers of the mercy God has given them!

FAITH. This gift is found listed in Romans 12:8-10. Perhaps, miraculous faith is in view. (Compare Matthew 17:20). I am convinced, however, that this is the ability to manifest complete and implicit trust and confidence in God in respect of His power and love working providentially in every detail of our life, supplying all of our needs and guiding all our steps. God give us the faith of Proverbs 3:5-6, "*Trust in Jehovah with all thy heart, and lean not upon thine own understanding: In all thy ways acknowledge him, and he will direct thy paths.*"

While it is true that God is not today supplying the church with miraculous powers, it is just as true that God is supplying the church with everything that is necessary to its growth, development, work, worship and discipline through His Word and His ministers. We need to rely less on our own ability and more on the help that is at our disposal.

> Be not wise, in thine own eyes; fear Jehovah, and depart from evil: It will be health to thy naval, and marrow to thy bones. Honor Jehovah with thy substance, and with the first-fruits of all thine increase: So shall thy barns be filled with plenty, and thy vats shall overflow with new wine (Proverbs 3:7-10).

> And my God shall supply every need of yours according to his riches in glory in Christ Jesus. Now unto our God and Father be the glory for ever and every. Amen." (Philippians 4:19-20).

> "Now unto him that is able to do exceeding abundantly above all that we ask or think, according to the power that worketh in us, unto him be the glory in the church and in Christ Jesus unto all generations for ever and ever. Amen. (Ephesians 3:20-21).

> And God is able to make all grace abound unto you: that ye, having all sufficiency in everything, may abound unto every good work . . . And he that supplieth seed to the sower and bread for food, shall supply and multiply your seed for sowing and increase the fruits of your righteousness: ye being enriched in everything unto all liberality, which worketh through us thanksgiving to God (2 Corinthians 9:8, 10-11).

Now unto him that is able to guard you from stumbling, and to set you before the presence of his glory without blemish in exceeding joy, to the only God our Saviour, through Jesus Christ our Lord, be glory, majesty, dominion, and power, before all time, and now, and for evermore. Amen (Jude 24-25).

QUESTIONS

Chapter Seven

1. List and discuss some spiritual gifts given to the church which are not miraculous and temporary.

2. The gift of teaching is considered to be one of the major and most desirable gifts in the church today. Discuss what is required to obtain and maintain this gift.

3. Since some in the church have the gift of evangelism, does this indicate that others have no responsibility in teaching others the gospel?

4. Discuss this statement: "While everyone has the gift to give to some degree, not everyone has the ability to do so with singleness of heart." Does this mean that some may give grudgingly and yet their gift is acceptable to God?

THE HOLY SPIRIT OF GOD
AND THE CHRISTIAN

Introduction

The relationship that the individual Christian sustains to the Holy Spirit of God is not only one of the grandest themes presented in the New Testament, but one of the most prominent. Manifold passages (which we will consider in this chapter) show a very personal relation between God's children and God's Spirit.

We have already seen in previous chapters that God's Spirit had been actively concerned with His people. He had inspired all of the scriptures, Old and New covenants; He had led Israel out of captivity and given them rest in their land (Isaiah 63:1-14); He had empowered them to build the tabernacle (Exodus 31:1-5) and then to rebuild the temple (Zechariah 4:6-9). Jesus summed it all up when he said, "*He hath been with you, but shall be in you*" (John 14:17). The Holy Spirit had been with them, strengthening, leading and empowering them; but, now, He was to take up his abode within them.

Jesus had, during his personal ministry, prophesied a new era in which all the believers would be recipients of God's Spirit:

Now on the last day, the great day of the feast, Jesus stood and cried, saying, If any man thirst, let him

*come unto me and drink. He that believeth on me, as
the scriptures hath said, from within him shall flow
rivers of living water. But this spake he of the Spirit,
which they that believed on him were to receive: for
the Spirit was not yet given: because Jesus was not yet
glorified"* (John 7:37-39).

The words, *"for the Spirit was not yet given,"* cannot be
understood in their absolute sense, because many passages
indicate that the Spirit had been given in the sense of being
with them to empower, lead or influence in some other way.
The context of John 7 indicates that Jesus is talking about an
abiding, indwelling of the Holy Spirit. Notice, *"from within
him shall flow."* The original language reads, *"from out of his
belly shall flow."* That is indwelling with a vengeance. So Jesus
said that those who came to be continual believers in Him
would receive the Spirit of God to indwell their bodies, but
only after He had been glorified. (Compare Acts 2:33, 38-39.)
Then, in the farewell discourse with His apostles, Jesus said,

*And I will pray the Father, and he shall give you
another Comforter, that he may be with you for ever,
even the Spirit of truth; whom the world cannot
receive; for it beholdeth him not, neither knoweth
him; ye know him; for he **abideth with** you, and **shall
be in you**. I will not leave you desolate: I come unto
you* (John 14:16-18).

Jesus said the apostles' relationship to the Spirit of God
was going to change – something new was going to occur. The
Spirit has been "with" them, in the person of Jesus, but now He
was going to be "in" them. So twice in the book of John, Jesus
promises that men, all believers (in John 7:38-39) and the
apostles (in John 14:16-18) would receive the Holy Spirit as an
abiding, indwelling guest.

In the book of Acts, Luke records two statements from Peter that show these statements of Jesus were fulfilled in the lives of individual Christians. In Acts 2:38-41 we read,

> *Repent ye, and be baptized every one of you in the name of Jesus Christ unto the remission of your sins; and ye shall receive the gift of the Holy Spirit. For to you is the promise* (of the Holy Spirit, Acts 2:33), *and to your children, and to all that are afar off, even as many as the Lord our God shall call unto him. And with many other words he testified, and exhorted them, saying, Save yourselves from this crooked generation. They then that received his word were baptized; and there were added unto them in that day about three thousand souls."*

Then in Acts 5:32, "*And we* (the apostles) *are witnesses of these things; and so is the Holy Spirit, whom God hath given to them that obey him.*" Thus, Peter teaches that all those who obey God – who repent of their sins and are baptized for their remission – receive God's gift, the Holy Spirit of God.

It is in the epistles of Paul, particularly, that we learn not only the fact of the indwelling but also the function of the indwelling Spirit of God. Let us notice one by one the different emphases that Paul makes.

THE GIFT OF GOD. In agreement with Acts 2:38 and 5:32, Paul says that God had given the Galatian Christians the Spirit as they heard the word of faith, obeyed it and became His sons (Galatians 3:2, 5, 26-29; 4:6). To the Corinthians he said, "*Know ye not that your body is a temple of the Holy Spirit ... which ye have from God*" (1 Corinthians 6:19). And, finally, Paul said: "*Therefore he that rejecteth, rejecteth not man, but God, who giveth His Holy Spirit unto you*" (1 Thessalonians

4:8). Thus the Holy Spirit of God is to Paul God's gift to His children.

THE SEAL OF GOD UNTO SALVATION. Three passages mention this function of the Spirit.

> *Now he that establisheth us with you in Christ, and anointed us, is God; who also sealed us, and gave us the earnest of the Spirit in our hearts* (2 Corinthians 1:21-22).

> *In whom* (i.e. Christ), *having also believed, ye were sealed with the Holy Spirit of promise* (Ephesians 1:13).

> *And grieve not the Holy Spirit of God, in whom ye were sealed unto the day of redemption* (Ephesians 4:30).

Sealing the Christians is not a work of the Spirit. It is the work that the Father accomplishes by giving the Spirit to the Christians – the Father is the Sealer and the Spirit is the seal. The idea of these passages is a simple one. The word "seal" means "to set a mark upon by the impress of a seal, to stamp, to confirm, authenticate" (Thayer, page 609). Thus, God has approved us as being His by giving us His Spirit. John says, *"Hereby we know that we abide in him and he in us, because he hath given us of his Spirit"* (1 John 4:13). Someone might ask, "But how do we know that we have the Spirit as our seal?" We have God's word for it, and therefore by a knowledge of that word and faith in Christ, we believe it as surely as we believe we have remission of sins when we repent and are baptized in the name of Christ (Acts 2:38).

THE EARNEST OF OUR INHERITANCE. This is the second thing that Paul says the Spirit is to the Christians. *"Who (God) also sealed us and gave us the earnest of the Spirit in* *our hearts"* (2 Corinthians 1:22); *"Now he that wrought us for this very thing is God, who gave us the earnest of the Spirit"* (2 Corinthians 5:5); *"Which* (the Spirit) *is an earnest of our inheritance, unto the redemption of God's own possession, unto the praise of His glory"* (Ephesians 1:14). The word earnest means "money which in purchases is given as a pledge that the full amount will subsequently be paid" (Thayer, page 75). Thus, the Spirit is God's pledge to us that one day we will be full recipients of all His glory (Cf. Romans 8:23; Philippians 3:20-21). Praise God for the abundant assurance that He has given us in His Spirit! Notice again this is what the Spirit is to us, not what He does for us. The Spirit, Himself, is the earnest that God has given us in our hearts.

MOTIVATION TO GODLY LIVING. The faith that the Christian has of the presence of the Spirit within is one of the greatest incentives to godliness that we possess. In 1 Corinthians chapter six Paul is pleading with the brethren not to return to a life of fornication but to flee from it. He uses several wonderful arguments and then concludes by saying, *"Or know ye not that your body is a temple of the Holy Spirit which is in you, which ye have from God? and ye are not your own; for ye were bought with a price: glorify God therefore in your body"* (1 Corinthians 6:19-20). The knowledge of the Spirit's indwelling was the power that was to enable these Christians to flee fornication. I have personally known alcoholics that have conquered the desire to drink because of the knowledge of God's gift within them.

PURITY OF LIFE is a result Paul lists of "walking by the Spirit" in Galatians 5:16-17. There is a warfare, Paul says, between my flesh and my spirit. My flesh desires satisfaction at any cost, even my soul's damnation. My spirit desires to fulfill God's will. It is only by the Spirit's help that I can fulfill my spirit's desire. By comparing this passage with 1 John 1:7, we can see that as I direct my steps by the light of God's word the Spirit helps me in overcoming the flesh.

LIBERTY FROM LEGALISM results from being led by the Spirit, according to Galatians 5:18. Those who live under a system of grace live where sin no longer has dominion (Romans 6:14). When the Spirit leads us (through the Word) to trust in Jesus as our Saviour and Sin-offering, we are freed from the death struggle of legal law-keeping; and we are given the power and the inclination to work in a more significant way than ever before. (Compare 1 Corinthians 15:10). Praise God for the system of Grace!

UNITY BETWEEN BRETHREN comes about by walking by the Spirit's direction (Galatians 5:25). When there is disunity and hatred between brethren, it is proof positive that there is no respect for the Spirit of God and His direction through the revealed word. The word translated "walk" in this verse means "to proceed in a row, go in order" (Thayer, page 589). It would best be translated "march." Thus, Paul is saying that the Spirit of God calls the cadence to which we march. Those out of step are to be withdrawn from (2 Thessalonians 3:6ff).

THE SOURCE OF OUR SPIRITUAL LIFE. In every letter Paul teaches this fact. The Holy Spirit helps our infirmities (Romans 8:26). It is through the power of the Spirit that we abound in hope (Romans 15:13). It is by the power of the Spirit that we are sanctified (Romans 15:16; 2 Thessalonians 2:13-14). Paul lists the terrible past life of the immoral Corinthians in 1 Corinthians 6:9-11, but now they are washed, they are sanctified, they are justified in the name of Jesus and by the Spirit of our God.

THE ATMOSPHERE IN WHICH WE LIVE. It is easy to see that to Paul the great actions and qualities of the

Christian life are all in the Spirit. The Kingdom of God is righteousness, peace and joy in the Holy Spirit (Romans 14:17). We pray in the Spirit (Ephesians 6:18). Christians love each other in the Spirit (Colossians 1:8). Even in the midst of persecution we can have joy in the Holy Spirit (1 Thessalonians 1:6). The worship of the Christian is shared and offered in the Spirit (Philippians 3:3). Life in the Spirit is the only atmosphere and climate in which godly qualities can grow and in which Christian graces can ripen.

THE EVER-PRESENT REPRESENTATIVE OF THE GODHEAD. This great truth is emphasized in Ephesians 2:22: *"In whom ye also are builded together for a habitation of God in the Spirit."* John agrees, *"And he that keepeth his commandments abideth in him and he in him. And hereby we know that he abideth in us, by the Spirit which he gave us"* (1 John 3:24). Jesus promised His apostles that He would come back to them in the presence of the Comforter the Holy Spirit (John 14:16-18); and when He had thus come back He would be with them always *"even to the end of the world"* (Matthew 28:20). As long as a person possesses the Spirit of God, he belongs to Christ and Christ dwells in his heart through the Spirit (Romans 8:9; Ephesians 2:16-17).

Two other works of the Spirit need to be covered in detail. One of these is His work of interceding for the Christian (Romans 8:26-27). Hardeman Nichols' work on this subject in the Fort Worth Christian College Lectures in 1964 is an outstanding one. There is no way I can improve on Hardeman's work, so I include it here verbatim.

The Intercession of the Holy Spirit

When approaching a study of the magnitude of this lectureship, one is led into a fuller knowledge of all the Godhead and into a richer appreciation of all that is provided for us by grace, especially that which pertains to the person and work of the Holy Spirit. Our lesson focuses attention upon one of the most encouraging of all the "exceeding great and precious promises" revealed in the Book of God:

> And in like manner the Spirit also helpeth our infirmity: for we know not how to pray as we ought; but the Spirit himself maketh intercession for us with groanings which cannot be uttered; and he that searcheth the hearts knoweth what is the mind of the Spirit, because he maketh intercession for the saints according to the will of God (Romans 8:26-27).

Whatever the meaning of the details of this declaration, one thing is evident from a casual reading: the Holy Spirit is deeply interested in the prayers and affairs of men. He is concerned about burdens and helps to bear them. Careful of the weaknesses of saints, the Spirit expresses their needs and pleads their cause before the Father. This intercession by the Holy Spirit is surely one of the most remarkable works performed in behalf of Christians.

What Is Intercession?

Derivation. Intercession has its origin in a Greek word meaning, properly ". . . to light upon a person or a thing, fall in with, hit upon."[1] This term was derived from a word which meant to happen, chance."[2] Vine says the noun came to be a "technical term for approaching a king."[3]

(Westwood, N.J.: Revell, 1957), *enteuxis,* Intercessions, p. 267.

---

[1] Joseph H. Thayer, *A Greek-English Lexicon of the New Testament* (New York: Harper and Brothers, 1889), *entunchano,* p. 219.

[2] Thayer, ibid., *tuncano,* p. 632.

[3] W. E. Vine, *Expository Dictionary of New Testament Words*

Occurrences in Scriptures

The Greek word for intercession occurs in the New Testament in all its forms eight times. It is translated "prayer" in 1 Timothy 4:5 and "intercessions" in 1 Timothy 2:1. The other six times it occurs in verb form and is translated "dealt with" in Acts 25:24, the remainder of times in the King James it is "make intercession" (the American Standard has "pleadeth against" in Romans 11:2). The intercessory works of Christ and the Spirit are mentioned twice each: Romans 8:34 and Hebrews 7:25 and our text.

Definition of Intercession

Intercession means, "seeking the presence and hearing of God on behalf of others."[4] The verb means to meet with in order to converse; then, to make petition. . . plead with a person, either for or against others; (a) against, Acts 25:24. . . against Paul; in Romans 11:2, of Elijah . . . against Israel; (b) "for," in Romans 8:27, of the intercessory work of the Holy Spirit for the saints."[5] Romans 8:26 uses the same word from the Greek for intercession, but prefixes it with "*huper*," "on behalf of," to show that the petition of the Holy Spirit is on behalf of and not against the saints. Bullinger[6] says intercession means, "requests concerning others and on their behalf."

Examples of Intercessions to God

Man for Man.

---

[4] W. E. Vine, ibid., *enteuxis,* p 267, Intercessions
[5] W. E. Vine, ibid., *entunchano,* p 267, Intercessions B Verbs
[6] Ethelbert W. Builinger, *A Critical Lexicon and Concordance to the English and Greek New Testament* (London: Lamp Press, 8th ed., 1957), p. 416.

One of the earliest examples of man's interceding for man is recorded in Genesis 18:23-32. Upon hearing of the Lord's plan to destroy the cities of the plain,

Abraham drew near, and said, Wilt thou consume the righteous with the wicked? Peradventure there are fifty righteous within the city: wilt thou consume and not spare the place for the fifty righteous that are therein? That be far from thee to do after this manner, to slay the righteous with the wicked, that so the righteous should be as the wicked: that be far from thee: shall not the Judge of all the earth do right? And Jehovah said, If I find in Sodom fifty righteous within the city, then I will spare all the place for their sake. And Abraham answered and said, Behold now, I have taken upon me to speak unto the Lord, who am but dust and ashes: peradventure there shall lack five of the fifty righteous: wilt thou destroy all the city for the lack of five? And he said, I will not destroy it, if I find there forty and five.

With persistent pleading, Abraham lowers the figure of righteous "salt" to forty, then thirty, and twenty, to ten. Thus Abraham, the father of the Jews, demonstrates a quality which has often been attributed to his seed as one of their outstanding traits. Could it be that the phrase "jewing down," originated upon the occasion of Abraham's persuasive intercession for Sodom? If God was willing to spare wicked Sodom through another's intercession if ten righteous could be found there, we are convinced from the beginning of this study that such is beneficial.

Another example of intercession by man for man is found in Exodus 32:7-14 when the Israelites made a golden calf while Moses was receiving the law on Mount Sinai. God was ready to consume that "stiff-necked people;" but Moses pleaded for their lives and God accepted his entreaty.

Job interceded for his "friends" in Job 42:8-9 at the command of God and Paul made a plea for Israel in Romans 10:1-4.

The New Testament commands Christians to make requests concerning others. *"I exhort, therefore, first of all, that supplications, prayers, intercessions, thanksgivings, be made for all men . . ."* (1 Timothy 2:1). James 5:16 commands, *"pray one for another."*

When Peter was imprisoned by Herod, *"Prayer was made earnestly of the church unto God for him"* (Acts 12:5). Their prayers were intercessions. Stephen even interceded for his murderers in Acts 7:60, beseeching, *"Lord, lay not this sin to their charge."*

<u>Christ for the saints.</u>

In addition to man's intercessions for man, the Bible tells of the work of Christ for the saints in this respect. Besides His other functions, Christ *". . . also maketh intercession for us"* (Romans 8:34). Hebrews 7:25 declares *"he ever liveth to make intercession for them"* (who *"draw near unto God through him"*).

John uses another term which is synonymous to intercessor, when, in 1 John 2:1 he calls Christ our "Advocate." Literally, this word means, called to one's side, i.e., to one's aid . . . It was used in a court of justice to denote a legal assistant, counsel for the defense, an advocate; then, generally, one who pleads another's cause, an intercessor . . ."[7]

---

[7] W. E. Vine, ibid., *parakletos*, p. 208, Comforter

Holy Spirit for the saints.

A similar intercessor work is performed for us by the Holy Spirit. Besides the statements in our text, the Spirit is called the "Comforter," (John 14:26), where the same Greek word is used which is translated "Advocate" in 1 John 2:1. Since the word means an intercessor we can see why Jesus chose to call the Spirit "another Comforter," for both the Spirit and Jesus do the work of a Paraclete.

Some have been inclined to limit the work of the Holy Spirit as Comforter to the apostles through His miraculous influences upon them; but Jesus said, *"I will pray the Father, and he shall give you another Comforter, that he may be with you for ever"* (John 14:16). Luke also says that following the conversion of Paul, *"the church throughout all Judaea and Galilee and Samaria had peace, being edified; and, walking in the fear of the Lord and in the comfort of the Holy Spirit, was multiplied"* (Acts 9:31). "Comfort" in this passage is from the same word meaning "an intercessor" which is translated "Comforter" in John 14 and "Advocate" in 1 John 2. Hence, the intercession of the Spirit was known by the early church as a source of comfort and aid to them in their rapid growth. The assistance of the Spirit's intercession can help us in the same way now.

Mediation Distinguished from Intercession
Holy Spirit Intercedes, Not Mediates

The Holy Spirit performs the work of interceding for the saints, while Christ both intercedes and mediates. *"For there is one God, one mediator also between God and men, himself man, Christ Jesus, who gave himself a ransom for all; the testimony to be borne in its own times"* (1 Timothy 2:5, 6).

There can be many intercessors; but there is only one mediator and He is Christ.

Mediation of Christ Distinguished from
Intercession of Holy Spirit

Let us not confuse the work of the Spirit in intercession with the work of Christ as our one mediator. There are at least five distinctive features which will help us to see the difference.

First, our Lord as mediator stands "between God and men" 1 Timothy 2:5. Mediator is derived from a Greek term whose root means, "middle."[8] Hence, a mediator is "one that acts between two parties; . . ."[9] The intercessor stands by the side of one to plead his case to another. We have already seen this idea is inherent in both *intercede and Comforter.*

Second, a mediator belongs to two parties while an intercessor represents one party to another. Paul argued, *"Now a mediator is not a mediator of one"* (Galatians 3:20). Jesus perfectly qualified in this respect and one of His favorite expressions to denote himself was, "Son of man" (Matthew 16:13), yet he was also "Son of God" (v. 16).

Third, a mediator "is a sponsor or surety;"[10] hence he must interpose some offering of surety or guarantee. Christ "gave himself" as a ransom for all (1 Timothy 2:6). "Through his own blood" (Hebrews 9:12), he serves as the "mediator of the new covenant" (Hebrews 12:24). An intercessor pleads and makes petition on behalf of another; but his work does not include making a surety.

---

[8] Greek, *mesos.*

[9] *The Analytical Greek Lexicon* (New York: Harper and Brothers), *mesites,* p. 264.

[10] Thayer, ibid., p. 401, *mesiteuo 2.*

Fourth, a mediator is for enemies, while the intercession of the Holy Spirit is "for the saints" (Romans 8:27). Thayer defines a mediator as "one who intervenes between two, either to make or restore peace and friendship . . ."[11] The apostle Paul defines this work of our one mediator in 2 Corinthians 5:19-21: *"To wit, that God was in Christ reconciling the world unto himself . . ."* To reconcile means to restore to friendship and God was doing this through Christ's mediation.

Some intercessions are made by man for those who are lost, as Paul prayed for Israel in Romans 10:1-4, not that they would be saved in their sins or that the gospel would be ignored, but that they would accept God's plan for making man righteous. Man makes intercessions for all men (1 Timothy 2:1); but this is not true of the Holy Spirit. He "maketh intercession for us" "for the saints" (Romans 8:26, 27).

Fifth, a mediator must ratify his covenant. Thayer says in defining it, one who intervenes between two, . . .to form a compact, or for ratifying a covenant . . ."[12] The book of Hebrews emphasizes that Christ is the mediator of the new covenant.[13] Salvation is offered upon the terms of His covenant and He, ". . . *would have all men to be saved, and come to the knowledge of the truth. For there is one God, one mediator also between God and men, himself man, Christ Jesus"* (1 Timothy 2:4, 5).

The intercession of the Holy Spirit is according to the terms of Christ's ratified covenant. Romans 8:27 says, *"He maketh intercession for the saints according to the will of God."*

---

[11] Thayer, ibid., p. 401, *mesites.*
[12] Thayer, ibid., p. 401, *mesites.*
[13] Hebrews 8:6; 9:15; 12:24.

Example of Distinction Between
Intercession and Mediation

Having seen these five distinguishing factors, may we over-simplify the matter, and present an example which will help us to see the difference between intercession and mediation. Let us suppose that a man owes a debt of one million dollars and he cannot repay the sum. His friends are interested in him and they approach the banker and entreat him to lend the needed capital. When asked if they are able to supply collateral, they must say they do not have the ability to guarantee the note. A rich man sees the debtor's plight, goes to the banker and furnishes his own possessions as surety, declaring, "I'll sign the note." While the other friends could only plead his cause and thus intercede for him, this rich man had represented the interests both of the banker in providing the collateral and of the debtor by signing his note. He was therefore serving as a mediator.

Our illustration will not fit every detail of the distinction; but it will help us to see there is no contradiction in the Scriptures when it declares there is only one mediator and many intercessors.

Some Deductions from the Text

Turning now from these things for a closer examination of the passages upon our subject, let us notice some valid conclusions which will define the great work of the Spirit about which we are concerned.

We Learn About the Holy Spirit

His person.

Plainly, the work of the Holy Spirit and His nature require that we see Him as a personality and not a mere essence. Romans 8:26, 27 tells two things about Him which require personality. It is stated that He has "mind." Also we see that the Spirit is not the same personality as the Father although they are united in purposes; hence, "one" in harmony and nature while distinct in person. *"He that searcheth the hearts* (one personality) *knoweth what is the mind of the Spirit,* (another personality) *because he maketh intercession for the saints."* The Father and Spirit are distinct persons, for the Spirit certainly is not interceding to Himself!

His character.

This intercessory work performed in behalf of man by the Holy Spirit tells us about the great qualities of His divine character.

Rather than looking upon his office of intercession as a drudgery, the Holy Spirit loves His work. Jesus performs a similar work for us with joy. The book of Hebrews says, ". . . *he ever liveth to make intercession"* (7:25). That is, Christ enjoys interceding for us. When a mother *lives* for her children, it means they are her chief joy in life. Even the Greek term has this connotation. One of its definitions is, "to enjoy real life . . . this life in the absolute fullness Christ enjoys . . ."[14] And Christ said, ". . . *he shall give you another Comforter"* (John 14:16), meaning, "another of the same sort"[15] and possessing the same interest in interceding as does our Lord.

It should give us confidence to know that the Spirit is concerned about man and desires to help him with his weaknesses and intercede for him to God. The "*-eth*" ending on the verbs in the King James Bible shows that the Spirit is constant in this aid. He "helpeth our infirmity" and "maketh

---

[14] Thayer, ibid., p. 270, *zao.*

[15] W. E. Vine, ibid., p. 208, Comforter, parakletos: "another *(allos, another of the same sort, not heteros,* different) Comforter."

intercession for us" (both present indicative) showing that we can depend upon Him, who, like the Father, is "a very present help in trouble" (Psalm 46:1).

He respects the will of God. If He were devoid of this trait, He would not be flawless; so verse 27 says, *"He maketh intercession for the saints according to the will of God."* It is God's will to hear saints and reject the prayers of the rebellious as "abomination" (Proverbs 28:9). Sin separates us from God so that He will not hear (Isaiah 59:1, 2). *"If I regard iniquity in my heart, the Lord will not hear,"* said David in Psalm 66:18. In the New Testament, Peter quotes, *"The eyes of the Lord are upon the righteous, and his ears unto their supplication: but the face of the Lord is upon* (against, AV) *them that do evil"* (1 Peter 3:12). With full respect of God's will upon this and every matter, the Spirit makes intercession for those who have likewise respected God's will. He intercedes for the saints.

We Are Taught About Affliction

The entire context is about the Christian and affliction. In the seventeenth verse, we read of the wonderful privileges belonging to saints with an inheritance of Heaven before them. But he no sooner describes this prospect than he presents the condition, notice, *". . . if so be that we suffer with him."*

Saints Not Exempt from Suffering and Affliction

Even saints, who compose the new creation of God, are not exempt from present woes and common frailties as long as they are in this world. They are surrounded by trials, encompassed by reminders of their own weaknesses, exposed to the bombardments of temptation, attacked by disease, and anguished by death and calamity. Even of the apostles, *"who have the first-fruits of the Spirit,"* Paul said, *"Even we ourselves groan within ourselves, waiting for our adoption, to wit, the redemption of our body"* (verse 23).

Heaven's Attitude Toward Our Sufferings

If we were left to bear all these things alone, we would be doomed; but our text declares that we receive help from the other side. *"And in like manner the Spirit also helpeth our infirmity."* This teaches us that the Holy Spirit *alleviates,* not *eliminates,* our infirmities. Of "helpeth," Guy N. Woods says, "This word is a compound verb, from *lambano,* to take hold of, *syn,* together, with and *anti,* on the opposite side, over against. It is of interest to observe that this verb occurs only one other time in the Greek Testament – in the narrative of Luke 10:40, when Martha, vexed and cumbered with much serving, and annoyed because of Mary's uncooperativeness, asked Jesus to bid Mary to help, *synantilabetai,* literally, to "Stand over on the opposite side from me, and take hold of the work, so that the two of us working together can get the job done!" Was Martha attempting to move a heavy table at the very moment she addressed these words to the Savior? Did she also point to the table when she requested Jesus to bid Mary to take hold on the other side and help her? We may well believe that such was so, for this is the picture drawn for us in the Greek verb. The Spirit helps us – He stands over against us, as it were, and lifts with us until by our united efforts our burdens are lifted."[16] Thus are our burdens lightened.

Afflictions have a purpose and God can turn them to benefit us. The Spirit realizes this and we should notice His teaching in the Scriptures upon this truth. Although the affliction may originate as a "messenger of Satan," God can make it work in such a way that its result is for good, as in the case of Paul's affliction in 2 Corinthians 12:7-10. Its purpose, said Paul, was *"that I should not be exalted overmuch."* It kept

---

[16] Guy N. Woods, *How To Use The Greek New Testament,* (Memphis, Tenn.: 1951), p. 61.

him humble. Although he besought the Lord three times to remove it, the answer to his prayers was, *"My grace is sufficient for thee: for my power is made perfect in weakness."* It was then that Paul learned the reason why afflictions are not entirely eliminated: *"When I am weak, then am I strong."*

Afflictions also develop patience and the eighth chapter of Romans stresses this virtue. Young's transliteration of verse nineteen pictures saints "on tiptoe to see the wonderful sight of the sons of God coming into their own."[17] But they must wait it out. *"If we hope for that which we see not, then do we with patience wait for it"* (verse 25). Our waiting is not in indifference, but one which suggests "welcoming"[18] – the way a child waits for a ship on which his mother is to arrive. In the meanwhile, saints patiently bear their infirmities in hope of better things, knowing, *"the sufferings of this present time are not worthy to be compared with the glory which shall be revealed to us-ward"* (verse 18). This prompted Paul to describe it as *"light affliction, which is but for a moment"* (2 Corinthians 4:17 – AV). *"We also rejoice in our tribulations: knowing that tribulation worketh patience,"* (Romans 5:3), when we see that the Godhead is seeking our *good,* not our *ease.*

The Saints' Attitude Toward Affliction

When taken into proper perspective, affliction is seen as a blessing in disguise. David said, *"Before I was afflicted I went astray; but now I observe thy word. . . . It is good for me that I have been afflicted; that I may learn thy statutes"* (Psalm 119:67, 71). Paul rejoiced in his suffering and he said, *"Wherefore I take pleasure in weaknesses, in injuries, in*

---

[17] J. B. Phillips, *Letters To Young Churches,* (N.Y.: MacMillan), p. 18.

[18] Thayer, ibid., p. 131, SYN., *dekomai with apek-*

necessities, in persecutions, in distresses, for Christ's sake" (2 Corinthians 12:10). All saints should rejoice, even in persecution (Matthew 5:12); because "*our light affliction which is but for a moment, worketh for us more and more exceedingly an eternal weight of glory*" (2 Corinthians 4:17). The Holy Spirit has promised to make life's sum and total good: "*And we know that to them that love God all things work together for good*" (Romans 8:28). Besides all this, we have the blessed promise of help from the Holy Spirit of God as he intercedes. Let us never allow temporal adversity to make us forgetful of our spiritual prosperity.

Groanings in Affliction

What are these groanings? They cannot be complainings, for that is forbidden. "*Neither murmur ye, as some of them murmured, and perished by the destroyer*" (1 Corinthians 10:10). These are, rather, "mute sighs, the expression of which is suppressed by grief, Romans 8:26, . . . which (from their nature) cannot be uttered ."[19]

These groanings are ours, not the Holy Spirit's. Man, in grief with an oppressed and burdened heart, does not, and often cannot, transform the desires of his own soul into audible words of prayer. Perhaps you have heard one with emotions too deep for words only cry, "Oh, Lord!" while others, with hearts swollen by grief, cannot give vent to any outward expression, and suppress all sound. If the Holy Spirit could do no more than groan also, it would be sympathy, perhaps, but not intercession.

The Holy Spirit has great power of expression. He gave us the Bible (2 Peter 1:21): surely He who inspired the apostles and expressed the mind of God to man has no difficulty in

---

[19] Thayer, ibid., p. 25, *alaletos,* unutterable.

expressing the desires of man to God! He has "mind" which means "to have understanding, be wise."[20] He knows the things of God (1 Corinthians 2:11). Therefore, He is able to intercede with the eloquence and wisdom of God when we sigh.

Twice Paul states that these groanings are not uttered, but are "within ourselves." This is not to condemn audible crying and tears: there is a place for such. Even our Lord, ". . . *in the days of his flesh . . . offered up prayers and supplications accompanied by strong* (loud) *crying and tears*" (Hebrews 5:7). But Paul is emphasizing that our afflictions do not have to be accompanied with audible words or loud stentorian wails before the attention of the Holy Spirit is attracted to our needs. He lends his assistance and sustains us, even when we inwardly sigh.

We Are Enlightened About Prayer

✱ We are limited. That is a reason for prayer.

Man, in the midst of all his limitations, should be encouraged to know that acceptable prayer does not depend on the ability of the suppliant to express all needs in words. We are limited in *wisdom* and often we do not know *"what"* (AV) or *"how"* (ASV) *"to pray as we ought."* Sometimes we do not know what we *need,*— but there are times when we see we are in deep need of help from the Lord, and we do not know what we *want.* The heart, at these times of deepest extremity, may not be able to break forth into ardent desires clothed in eloquence. The shell of words is removed and we only sigh. These unuttered groans the Spirit of God understands perfectly and translates into wise and good requests in our behalf, adequate for all our needs.

---

[20] Thayer, ibid., p. 658, *phroneo,* mind.

The *fact* of the intercession of the Holy Spirit is revealed in the Bible, but the *details* of how He does it are not. Suffice it for mortal mind to accept the fact, knowing that we are not equipped to understand all about the Godhead. If we did, we would be Gods ourselves. Ours is a life of trust: "*we walk by faith, not by sight*" (2 Corinthians 5:7). And we have complete confidence in the Spirit to fulfill His work. Remember, the intercession of the Holy Spirit is a work done *for* us, not to us. It is not something that is "better felt than told."

Our *limitations* are not the *limits* of our prayers.

Acceptable prayers are not limited to what we ask or think. We pray to God who is not limited. Let us declare with the Three Hebrews, "*Our God whom we serve is able*" (Daniel 3:17). He is "*able to do exceeding abundantly above all that we ask or think*" (Ephesians 3:20). He answers our own requests (Luke 11:9); but He is able to do exceeding abundantly above that! He accepts others' prayers in our behalf. Paul knew this and he wrote Philemon from prison to get him a room ready for he had that much confidence in the effectiveness of Philemon's intercession for him: "*But withal prepare me also a lodging: for I hope that through your prayers I shall be granted unto you*" (Philemon 22). If the intercessions of a man meant that much, how much more powerful must be the intercession of Christ and the Holy Spirit! This should cause us to pray "*at all seasons in the Spirit*" (Ephesians 6:18).

Conclusion

There is an old Western tale of a man who came out of the desert with his lips parched and dry and his tongue swollen, crying for water. As they cared for him and looked at his blistered skin, one man inquired if he had found no shade out in the desert. "Yes," he replied, "but I couldn't get into it." When asked why he couldn't get into it, he sagely said, "Did you ever try to get into your own shadow?" And so, many a man, away from his Maker, is traveling the barren wastelands of sin and materialism, seeking refuge in his own shadow, and finding no help, no aid. In the blistering day of suffering, he cries out and is mocked by the echo of his lonely wail. In search of some shelter, he crouches on the edge of his own shadow for protection from the blasting of the wind-borne sand of retribution and judgment, and finds no escape. Yet here, within reach of all humanity, is a place of refuge, like an oasis in the desert, where man, deluded by mirages of allurement in sin and degradation, can find shelter in the shadow of the cross of Christ and the constant care of his love. Revived and forgiven, encouraged by the knowledge of help and intercession on every side, he is ready to go forth anew toward that city which hath the foundations, whose builder and maker is God. *"The Lord is thy shade upon thy right hand. The sun shall not smite thee by day, nor the moon by night. The Lord shall preserve thee from all evil: he shall preserve thy soul. The Lord shall preserve thy going out and thy coming in from this time forth, and even for evermore"* (Psalm 121:5-8).

The church today can be like it was in Acts 9:31: "...*walking in the fear of the Lord and in the comfort of the Holy Spirit, was multiplied.*" Comfort is the result of intercession, and Luke declares that the Spirit's interceding comforted and blessed the church. No wonder it grew!

What a blessed consolation! While we face tribulation, or distress, or persecution, or famine, or nakedness or peril, or sword, or any common frailty of man, the Holy Spirit intercedes for us, allays our groans, falls in beside us and helps us lift our burdens, and strengthens us for the remainder of the journey home.

FILLED WITH THE SPIRIT. Being "filled with the Spirit" was many times the experience of the early church (Acts

4:32; 13:52; 6:3). In Ephesians 5:18-19 Paul admonishes the brethren, *"And be not drunken with wine, wherein is riot, but be filled with the Spirit; speaking one to another in psalms and hymns and spiritual songs."* In a parallel passage Paul admonishes, *"Let the word of Christ dwell in you richly; in all wisdom teaching and admonishing one another with psalms and hymns and spiritual songs, singing with grace in your hearts unto God"* (Colossians 3:16). By comparing these few passages we find that the Spirit can fill (influence and control) us to the degree that we let the word of Christ dwell in us. This should not be thought of as some mystical, mysterious, ecstatic experience reserved for the select few who discover the secret. This should be the experience of every child of God. Why is not the Holy Spirit the domineering force in our lives? Because we do not know His will, or because, if we do, we ignore it in favor of our own. Only by meditating day and night on what He wants us to do and say will we replace our desires with His desires. We shall find it necessary to often spend time reading and praying over His will in our lives conscious all the while that He is in us to aid us in fulfilling His purposes for us.

In summary we might say that the Holy Spirit of God does the following things for us:

1.   He strengthens us with power in our inner man – Ephesians 3:16.

2.   He enables Christ to dwell in our hearts by faith – Ephesians 3:17.

3.   He yearns for us and gives us the greater grace – James 4:5-6.

4.   He helps our infirmities and intercedes for us – Romans 8:26-27.

5. He helps us in overcoming sin – Romans 8:13; Galatians 5:16-17.

6. He makes us free from law and legalism as a system – Galatians 5:18.

7. He enables us to live in unity with our brethren – Galatians 5:25.

8. He enables us to bear fruit – Galatians 5:22.

9. He transforms our characters into God's likeness – 2 Corinthians 3:17-18.

10. He enables us to live in an atmosphere of holiness – Romans 14:17.

QUESTIONS

Chapter Eight

1. Describe the activity and the relationship the Spirit had with God's people under the Old Covenant.

2. What statement did Jesus make which would indicate a change of relationship between the Holy Spirit and God's people.

3. What relationship does the Holy Spirit now have with all obedient believers according to John 7:37-39; 14:16-18; Acts 2:38-41; Acts 5:32, etc.?

4. Discuss what it means to be sealed with the Holy Spirit. Does the Holy Spirit seal us?

5. Discuss how faith that the Holy Spirit's presence in us motivates to godly living.

6.   How does the indwelling Holy Spirit affect unity or disunity between brethren?

7.   In what way is the Holy Spirit involved in the Christian's spiritual life?

8.   Give the meaning of intercession and how and when the Holy Spirit intercedes on behalf of Christians.

9.   Discuss three examples of intercessions to God.

10. What differences do you see between intercession and mediation? What relationship do they have in the Christian life?

11. Discuss in detail heaven's attitude toward the suffering of Christians. Consider the purpose of suffering from heaven's view.

12. What should be the saint's attitude toward suffering and affliction? Support your answer with Scripture.

13. Explain the "groaning" spoken of in Romans 8:26. Who is groaning and why?

14. At the end of this chapter are ten things the Holy Spirit does for us. Discuss these at length.

SINS AGAINST THE HOLY SPIRIT

Blasphemy Against the Holy Spirit

Blasphemy is an old sin. The creature has been condemned down through the centuries of time for speaking against the creator. In Leviticus 24 Moses is told by God that any and all blasphemers are to be stoned to death by the entire congregation (nation) of Israel. Compare also Isaiah 65:7; 2 Kings 19:6-22; 2 Samuel 12:14; Psalms 74:10-18; Ezekiel 35:12.

The New Testament also contains frequent warnings against the sin of blasphemy. *"For the name of God is blasphemed among the Gentiles because of you,"* Paul told the Christian Jews at Rome (Romans 2:24). Paul admonished Titus to teach Christian women *"to be sober-minded, chaste, workers at home, kind, being in subjection to their own husbands, that the word of God be not blasphemed"* (Titus 2:5). Christian workers need to be careful along this line: *"Let as many as are servants under the yoke count their own masters worthy of all honor, that the name of God and the doctrine be not blasphemed"* (1 Timothy 6:1).

When Jesus came into this world, He came to a world ruined by sin. The devil assailed Him with every temptation in every way he could as long as Jesus lived. Men, inspired by devilish purposes, reviled, slandered and blasphemed Him, and finally they crucified Him. The climax of their words against Jesus and His mission is found in the accusation that He was in league, on the same team, with the devil. Jesus replied to this charge with these words,

> *Every sin and blasphemy shall be forgiven unto men;* *but the blasphemy against the Spirit shall not be* *forgiven. And whosoever shall speak a word against* *the Son of man, it shall be forgiven him; but the* *blasphemy against the Holy Spirit, it shall not be* *forgiven him; neither in this world, nor in that which* *is to come* (Matthew 12:31-32).

In the following context Jesus appeals to them to either make the tree and fruit good or make them both evil; for they are to be judged by their idle words in the day of judgment. In Mark's account of this same incident we read,

> *Verily I say unto you, All their sins shall be forgiven* *unto the sons of man and their blasphemies wherewith* *they blaspheme: but whosoever shall blaspheme* *against the Holy Spirit hath never forgiveness, but is* *guilty of an eternal sin: because they said, He hath an* *unclean Spirit* (Mark 3:28-29).

Then in Luke's account we read, "*And whosoever shall speak a word against the Son of man, it shall be forgiven him, but unto him that blasphemeth the Holy Spirit it shall not be forgiven*" (Luke 12:10). What is this terrible sin of which Jesus speaks in these passages?

We need to always keep a passage in its context in order to understand it. Jesus had just cast a demon out of a man and had claimed to do so by the power of the Holy Spirit (Matthew 12:28). Now the crowd is discussing this great wonder. His friends offer this explanation: "*He is beside himself*" (Mark 3:21). They attempted to carry Jesus forcefully from the scene thinking him to be temporarily insane. They had thus spoken a word against the Son of man and upon thinking about the great miracle would undoubtedly repent and be forgiven. His enemies, the scribes, said: *"He hath Beelzebub, and, By the prince of the demons casteth he out the demons"* (Mark 3:22). Their words were not so much against the Son of man as against the Holy Spirit by whom Jesus was empowered (Matthew 12:28; Luke 4:17-19). Not being able to consider the miracle as from God, they will never be able to receive the testimony of Christ and believe Him to be their Saviour (John 20:30-31; 10:38).

Then, we also need to reflect upon another fact. All of the Jews' lives and all through their history God had been speaking to them, appealing to them, offering them His truth and His revelation. But they had so long shut their ears to that voice, refused that guidance, been blind to that truth, that when God Incarnate came to them, they utterly failed to realize who He was and to recognize Him, and even saw in Him the work of the devil. They had so long chosen their own way, the wrong way, that in the end, good seemed to them evil and evil seemed good. (Compare Isaiah 5:20). That is the blasphemy against the Holy Spirit. This attitude also makes forgiveness impossible. If a man cannot recognize goodness when he sees it, then he does not even know when he is sinning. If by his repeated acts of rejecting God's power and God's powerful word, he has reached this state, then repentance is impossible, because goodness has lost its fascination and evil has lost its horror. It is not God who has shut the door (if He had He could open it); the person who has reached this point has shut it on himself.

The above two points establish two other truths. First, the one man who has not reached this point is the man who can still say: "I hope I have not yet committed the sin of blaspheming

God's Spirit." No man who is aware of the fact that he is a sinner has reached this point.

Second, the one way that we can be sure that we never individually and personally reach this point is to keep ourselves sensitive to the voice of God. He who lives close to Christ, constant in prayer, diligent in the study of God's word, ever mindful of Him in whom he lives and moves and has his being, can never commit this sin, for such a man is always ready to listen to God's truth, and to recognize it when he sees it.

Lying to the Holy Spirit

This is the first sin of which we have any record in the early church. In Acts 5 Ananias and Sapphira conspire with one another to deceive the apostles and cause them to think that they were giving all of their possessions to the relieving of the needy in the church. Peter, in Acts 5:3, says that Satan had filled the heart of Ananias to lie unto the Holy Spirit and in verse 9 he tells Sapphira that she and her husband had conspired together to try the Holy Spirit of God. One wonders how many in the church today are deceiving the leaders into thinking that they are giving much more than they are. We need to remember the penalty for such a sin.

Resisting the Holy Spirit

This was the sin of the Jews down through the ages of their existence (Acts 7:51). The prophets had been sent by God time and again to call the Jews back to Him. The Jews had not only turned deaf ears to God's Spirit in the prophets, but had stoned these men to death. When one resists the word of God through Spirit-inspired men, he resists the Spirit of God. We need to be careful lest we be found guilty of fighting against God and His Spirit.

Quenching the Holy Spirit

This was the sin of the Thessalonians: *"Quench not the Spirit; despise not prophesyings"* (1 Thessalonians 5:19-20). This is the sin of counting lightly the activity of the Spirit in one's life. Today we no longer have the provisional miraculous gifts of the Spirit, and therefore this passage's primary teaching is no longer applicable. Yet today the Spirit gives gifts unto God's children of a permanent, non-miraculous kind (Romans 12:6-8). If the Spirit, for instance, gives a man the gift of obtaining and giving money for the support of the Lord's work, and he despises this gift and does not exercise it, then he despises the Spirit who gave him the gift. Let us be diligent to fulfill whatever work the Lord gives us with all the strength and ability He gives us.

Grieving the Holy Spirit

This sin mentioned in Ephesians 4:30 points up a truth that we sometimes ignore. God, Christ and the Holy Spirit are put to sorrow of heart and soul through our unbelief and disobedience (compare Isaiah 63:7ff). Paul says in Ephesians 4 that we can grieve the Spirit by our impure language (vs. 25, 29); by using bitter and angry words against others (v. 26); by stealing, laziness and refusing to work (v. 28). The little things of our day-by-day life are important. The Spirit indwells us, and when we forget this and begin to fuss and bicker, he is grieved (compare James 4:1-10).

Defiling the Temple Of the Holy Spirit

This can be done individually and congregationally. One defiles the temple of God, the church of God, through faction and division (1 Corinthians 3:16-17); and God has promised that he will destroy all those who cause this division. The temple of God which is your body must also not be defiled or destroyed by immorality and dissipation (1 Corinthians 6:19-20). Let all of us pledge to keep the temple of God's Spirit holy, congregationally and individually.

Doing Despite unto the Holy Spirit

This was the sin of the Hebrew Christians in turning away from Christ back to Judaism (Hebrews 6:4-6; 20:26-29). Be sure and read these passages. In Hebrews 6 we read that the Christians are *"partakers of the Holy Spirit."* Those who go back into the world *"hath done despite unto the Holy Spirit."* The words "hath done despite unto" mean "to use wanton insult toward." This is so close to blasphemy against the Spirit that it would probably take the Spirit Himself to define the difference. We need to exhort one another day by day so this will never occur in our life (Hebrews 10:24-25; 3:12-14).

In concluding our study of what the Spirit means to the Christian today, let us attempt to summarize all that we have said. Just what does the Spirit provide for the Christian and the church today?

A Message

Much of the preaching that one hears today lacks the power, to change the life. Many times it boils down to opinion, prejudice, trivialities (moving around on the periphery and not penetrating into the core of the problem). Much of the message of modern pulpits is but an expression of the doubts and questionings of the pulpiteer. It is considered unintellectual to be certain in some circles. Many of the sermons heard today are irrelevant, spending time answering questions which no one is asking or discussing problems which are remote to the ears of the hearers.

It is only the Spirit through the Spirit-inspired word that can save us from these dangers. We need to remember that God said long ago: *"Not by might, not by power; but by my Spirit"* (Zechariah 4:6). Paul put it all in one passage:

> *But abide thou in the things which thou hast learned and hast been assured of, knowing of whom thou hast learned them; and that from a babe thou hast known the sacred writings which are able to make thee wise unto salvation through faith which is in Christ Jesus.*

> *Every scripture inspired of God is also profitable for teaching, for reproof, for correction, for instruction which is in righteousness; that the man of God may be complete, furnished completely unto every good work* (2 Timothy 3:14-17).

Nothing other than the Spirit's word and His power behind it is needed in any pulpit in any church in any country or land in the whole world today or any other day.

The preacher may be a scholar, an administrator, an ecclesiastical statesman, a scintillating orator, a social reformer; but he is nothing unless he is a man of the Spirit. PREACH THE WORD.

An Accent of Certainty

It is only through the Spirit-inspired word that the church can quit saying "I think so" and begin to say "I know it is so." The difference between the modern church and the first-century church was that then things were seen to be black and white, whereas today they are seen only in shades of gray. The church is looking too much like the world for some of the people to tell the difference anymore. If the church will present to the world something unique and different from the tossing waves of man's wisdom, then, and only then, will it attract those adrift in their sins.

In a book called *If Winter Comes,* one of its characters makes the following statement:

"Man cannot live by bread alone, the churches tell him; but he says, 'I am living on bread alone, and doing well on it.' But I tell you, Hapgood, that plumb down in the crypt and abyss of every man's soul is a hunger, a craving for other food than this earthly stuff. And the churches know it; and instead of reaching down to him what he wants-light, light- instead of that, they invite him to dancing and picture-shows, and you're a jolly good fellow, and religion's a jolly good thing and no spoil-sport, and all that sort of latter-day tendency. Why, man, he can get all that outside the churches and get it better. Light! Light! He wants light, Hapgood. And the padres come down and drink beer with him, and watch boxing-matches with him, and dance Jazz with him, and call it making religion a Living Thing in the Lives of the People. Lift the hearts of the people to God, they say, by showing them that religion is not incompatible with having a jolly fine time. *And there's no God there that a man can understand for him to be lifted up to.* Hapgood, a man wouldn't care *what* he had to give up if he knew he was making for something inestimably precious. But he doesn't know. Light, light-that's what he wants; and the longer it's withheld the lower he'll sink. Light! Light!"

It is a shame that words like these can be found in a novel written in 1921 when the church today is on the brink of saying just the opposite. This is not a condemnation of social fellowship in the church; but it should serve as a reminder that these things can never answer the hunger of a broken heart or the searchings of a lost soul. No church dare face the needs of a generation adrift from its moorings with anything but the Spirit-inspired word lived out in the life of Spirit-filled men and proclaimed by them.

A Steadfast Growth and Development

This is true to the individual as seen in Jude 20-21: *"But ye, beloved, building yourselves on your most holy faith, praying in the Holy Spirit, keep yourselves in the love of God, looking for the mercy of our Lord Jesus Christ unto eternal life."* As we yield ourselves to God's control we will continue to grow and develop, even unto eternity. But the church as a whole can only advance through the Spirit's help: *"So the church throughout all Judea and Galilee and Samaria had peace, being edified; and, walking in the fear of the Lord and in the comfort of the Holy Spirit, was multiplied"* (Acts 9:31). No longer should we marvel at the multiplying growth of the early church when we find that it was a result of their reverencing Christ and being helped (comforted) by the Holy Spirit. The Spirit can help us today through His Word, the Word of God (Ephesians 6:17); through interceding on our behalf (Romans 8:26-27); by strengthening our inner man (Ephesians 5:16); and through providentially working in our behalf (Romans 8:28; Isaiah 63:7-14; Psalms 139:7-10). The church today can gain the Spirit's help and begin to multiply through study, prayer and work.

A Real Fellowship

Paul's prayer for the Corinthians illustrates that true fellowship is possible through the Spirit: *"The grace of the Lord Jesus Christ, and the love of God, and the communion of the Holy Spirit, be with you all"* (2 Corinthians 13:14). The word "communion" means the same as the word "fellowship"– a joint sharing or participating. Then in Ephesians 4:3 Paul speaks of "the unity of the Spirit," and in Galatians 5:25 it is by "living in the Spirit" that I can "walk (or march) by the Spirit."

Division is the characteristic of the natural, carnal man (1 Corinthians 3:1-3; Jude 19); unity is the characteristic of the Christian man (John 13:34-35; 1 John 4:7-21). The curious and distressing feature about some churches today is the amount of bickering and difference and dispute and often long-lasting bitterness which arises about matters of personal prestige and rights and place and position and the like. Nothing could better prove the absence of the Spirit (Jude 19).

Fellowship has been defined as "the joy of going through life hand in hand with the comrade of one's choice, sharing one another's burdens, stimulating one another's courage, doubling one another's sagacity, buckling on one another's armor, wearing one another's laurels, and easing one another's pain." Compare Philippians 1:27-2:4.

An Adequate Doctrine of Conversion

We are grateful today for the emphasis that is being placed on mass evangelism, for the great number of conversions that are the result of this emphasis. But there is the danger that conversion will be looked on as the end in and of itself. It is true that at conversion a man has a new relation to God and a new hope in life. But this is only the beginning of the journey. Conversion results in justification. Justification must issue in sanctification. Things which were once accepted with equanimity must now be regarded with horror. A new responsibility accompanies the new privilege of which he has now become aware. And unless the Holy Spirit daily fills him with power in his inward man as he learns more about the Word, then his conversion will lead nowhere but to disappointment, disillusionment and frustration. We must start by confronting a man with the cross, but we must go on to tell him of the Risen Christ, of the Holy Spirit and the new life they make possible. Then, and only then, will glorification be the final result (Romans 8:1-39).

A True Worship

There are two divine requirements for acceptable worship: the proper standard, the truth of God and the proper attitude, a worshipful and reverent spirit (John 4:23-24). Both of these are the result of the Spirit's activity in the world. The Spirit revealed, inspired and recorded the truth of God to lead us in worship. And if we are to sing, pray and worship acceptably we must be filled with the Spirit (Ephesians 5:18-21).

Rita Snowden tells of a worship service in the Church of England: "Hymn and psalm and prayer, and the quiet murmuring voice of the Vicar tended to take my thoughts out the windows into the morning sunlight and over the fields and far away. The pity is, it was all so harmless, so gentle, so proper. There was nothing to remind anyone of that Young Man who strode the countryside and talked with the country people of Galilee in burning words . . . The kind of man who leaves you restless ever afterwards until you have found His God, and learned to call Him 'Father,' too." Today's greatest spectator sport is worship services.

If the people came to worship in preparation and in expectation, if the preacher committed himself and his message to God and His Spirit (Proverbs 3:5-7), then, and not until then, the flood tides of power would be unloosed upon men.

Unification of Life

We divide our life into sacred and secular. One part is God's business; the other part is our business. In one we are aware of the presence of God; in the other we practically forget He exists. But life in the Spirit would mean that no part of life is not sacred. I believe that God has declared this fact throughout the pages of His book. In Exodus 31, God's Spirit enabled men to have the skill to work with metal and cloth and wood. In Romans 12:6-8 God gives men the ability to give and to show mercy, things that would be done day-by-day and every day. Since the Holy Spirit of God dwells in the heart of God's sons (Galatians 4:6), we are constantly practicing the presence of God. If a man lives aware of this fact he experiences a new unity of purpose in his life and every moment of his life becomes a sacred moment.

The Power to Cope with Life

The rising number of suicides in this country is proof that many are finding it impossible to cope with life's problems and failures. The Spirit of God gives the Christian all that is necessary to cope with whatever life can bring. This is what Peter had in mind in 2 Peter 1:3-4:

> *Seeing that his divine power hath granted unto us all things that pertain unto life and godliness, through the knowledge of him that called us by his own glory and virtue; whereby he hath granted unto us his precious and exceeding great promises; that through these ye may become partakers of his divine nature, having escaped the corruption that is in the world through lust.*

Notice the great provisions of God's divine power (the Holy Spirit). First, I now have provided for me through the word of God all that I need for life and godliness. Second, I have, through that power and knowledge, obtained the precious promises of God. Third, I have through these promises partaken of Christ's nature. And fourth, I have escaped the corruption of the world. In Galatians 5:16 Paul says, "*walk by the Spirit, and ye shall not fulfill the lusts of the flesh.*"

Yes, it is important that we have the "Spirit of Christ," the Holy Spirit, the third person of the Godhead, dwelling within us. If we do not, then we are none of his (Romans 8:9). Thus having the Spirit depends upon being a Christian, and successfully living the Christian life depends on having the Spirit. Are you one of His or none of His? In the judgment will Christ say to the Father concerning you, "Father, here is one of Mine"? Or will he have to deny you and say, "He is none of Mine"?

All men can have the Holy Spirit abiding in them and belong to Christ. God gives the Spirit to sons (Galatians 4:6). One becomes a son by believing and being baptized into Christ (Galatians 3:26-29). Will you accept God's truth today?

MAY "THE GRACE OF THE LORD JESUS CHRIST, AND THE LOVE OF GOD, AND THE COMMUNION OF THE HOLY SPIRIT, BE WITH YOU ALL."

QUESTIONS

Chapter Nine

1. What is the meaning of "blasphemy" as it relates to God, Jesus, and the Holy Spirit?

2. Explain two truths which indicate that a person has not blasphemed the Holy Spirit and can guard one's self from committing the sin of blasphemy against the Spirit?

3. List several ways one might sin against the Holy Spirit. Do you know anyone guilty of any of these?

4. The early church experienced multiplying growth as a result of their reverencing Christ and being helped by the Holy Spirit. How can the Holy Spirit help us today to accomplish this multiplying growth?

5. True fellowship is possible through the Holy Spirit. Explain how this can be.

6. What involvement does the Holy Spirit have in acceptable worship?

7. In what way can the Holy Spirit bring about unity in our lives?

APPENDIX ON JOHN 3:30-36

I.   Notice the pronouns.

    v. 30 *"He* must increase" – i.e. Jesus

    v. 31 *"He* that cometh from above" – i.e. Jesus

    v. 32 *"He* hath seen and heard and bears witness" – i.e. Jesus

    v. 33 *"His* witness" – i.e. Jesus'

    v. 34 *"He* whom God sent" – i.e. Jesus

    v. 34 *"He* giveth not the Spirit by measure" – i.e. Jesus

    v. 35 Father hath given "all things into *His* hand" – i.e. Jesus'

II.   Notice tense of verb "Giveth."

    A.   The verse in the Greek:

        ὃνν γὰρ ἀπέστειλεν ὁ θεός τὰ ῥήματα τοῦ θεοῦ λαλεί, οὐ λὰρ ἐκ μέτρου δίδωσιν τὸ πνεῦμα.

    B.   The Parsing of "Giveth." Third person, Singular number, Present tense, Indicative mood, Active voice.

        1.   Third Person – the person spoken of (he, she, or it).

        2.   Singular – only one person acting.

        3.   Present tense – Going on at the time under consideration.

        4.   Indicative mood (or mode) –

        "Only in the indicative mode in Greek do the tenses show time absolutely. The main idea of tense is the 'kind of action,' the state of action. Even in the indicative, time is a secondary idea. Continued action, or a state of in-completion, is denoted by the present tense – this kind of action is called *durative or linear*. The action of the verb is shown in progress, as going on." *Beginner's Grammar of the Greek New Testament* by Wm. Hershy Davis, page 25. "Tense is the quality of the verb which has to do with action, i.e., *time* of action and *kind* of action. As to *time* of action there are three possibilities: past, present, or future. As to *kind* of action there are (for present consideration) two possibilities, *linear or punctiliar*. *Linear* action is action regarded as a point (.), i.e. action contemplated as a single perspective. The present tense indicates *progressive* action at the *present* time. e.g. "he is loosing." *Essentials of New Testament Greek* by Ray Summers, page 11.

    5.   Active Voice – The subject of the sentence is doing the acting.

  C. Application of the above grammatical analysis. At the time that John wrote the book, the Spirit was being continually given not by measure (by Jesus or God). Compare Acts 2:33; 38-39; 5:32; John 7:38-39; 14:16-17, 26; 15:26; 16:7; Gal. 3:14; 4:6; 1 Cor. 6:19; 2 Cor. 1:21-22; et al.

III. Notice King James translation.

  A. "Unto him" is not in the Greek text at all.

  B. "God giveth" – "God" is not in four out of seven authorities cited by Berry's Interlinear Greek-English New Testament, and is not even inserted in Nestles' Text. But, even if it is the original text, the verse would read that God continually gives the Spirit not by measure.

IV. Notice various translations.

A. Revised Standard Version: "For it is not by measure that he gives the Spirit."

B. New American Standard Version: "For He gives the Spirit without measure."

C. New English Bible: "So measureless is God's gift of the Spirit."

D. Wuest's Expanded Translation: "for not by measure does he give the Spirit."

E. Helen Montgomery, The New Testament in Modern English: "God does not give the Spirit sparingly."

V. Application of verse.

A. Not too many believed the testimony of Jesus but John the apostle, writing several years after the glorification of Jesus, claims the giving of the Spirit by Jesus to all believers to be one of the proofs of His claim to be God's own Son and Prophet. See John 7:38-39 and Acts 2:33, 38-39.

B. This passage categorically states that Jesus (or God if the variant is accepted) does not give the Spirit by measure. This forever buries the measure theory. Furthermore, how could one have a "measure" of the Holy Spirit, a person? One either has the Holy Spirit or he has not (Romans 8:9). The reply usually is, *" I really mean a Measure of his power." But if this is what we mean, let us say what we mean!* There is enough confusion in the world without using expressions which are misleading, especially when we can just as easily leave them alone. There are those who confuse the power given by the Spirit and the Spirit himself. *Let us seek to determine when the scriptures speak of the Spirit as a gift and when it speaks of the gifts of the Spirit.*

APPENDIX ON "FIRE"

Symbolic of Judgment of Wicked Nation

1. Genesis 19:24 – Sodom and Gomorrah
2. Deuteronomy 9:3 – God's destruction of the Sons of Anak
3. Deuteronomy 13:12-18 – The wicked, idolatrous city to be burned with fire.
4. Deuteronomy 32:15-43 – Judgment on Israel for they forgot God.
5. Joshua 6:24 – Jericho to be utterly destroyed and all things burned with fire.
6. Joshua 8:8, 19 – Ai to be utterly destroyed and all things burned with fire.
7. Joshua 11:6, 9, 11 – Hazor was utterly destroyed and burned with fire.
8. Judges 1:8 – Jerusalem was taken and burned with fire.
9. 2 Kings 2:11 – Elijah goes to heaven in God's chariots of fire.
10. 2 Kings 6:17 – Elisha's servant sees God's Chariots of fire bring judgment on the Syrians.
11. Job 15:34 – Fire will consume the tents of the wicked (that take bribes).
12. Job 20:26 – A fire shall destroy all that is left of the wicked.
13. Psalms 11:5-6 – Fire, brimstone and smoke the portion of the wicked.
14. Psalms 18:6ff – A great psalm of judgment, many mentions of fire.
15. Psalms 21:9 – God's enemies to be put into a fiery furnace and devoured by fire.
16. Psalms 50:3-6 – God's judgment to be accomplished by fire.

17. Psalms 68:2 – The wicked perish as wax before the fire.

18. Psalms 78:21 – God brings Jacob into judgment by fire (Captivity).

19. Psalms 79:5ff – The nations that know not God judged by fire.

20. Psalms 83:14-18 – All of Israel's enemies to be pursued and destroyed.

21. Psalms 97:3ff – All idol worshiper judged by God's fiery judgments.

22. Isaiah 1:7 – Israel's cities are burned by fire.

23. Isaiah 5:24-25 – Judah judged for rejection of Jehovah.

24. Isaiah 9:5 – God's enemies' weapons fuel for God's fire.

25. Isaiah 10:16-19 – Judah to be destroyed for its self-trust.

26. Isaiah 26:11 – The adversaries of Jehovah to be destroyed by fire.

27. Isaiah 29:6 – Jerusalem to be destroyed by a flame of devouring fire.

28. Isaiah 30:27-33 – Assyria to be destroyed in the blast furnace of God.

29. Isaiah 31:9 – Assyria to be burned by the fire of Zion in the furnace of Jerusalem.

30. Isaiah 33:11-12 – The proud Assyrian shall burn like stubble.

31. Isaiah 33:13-15 – The sinners of Israel shall be destroyed with an everlasting burning.

32. Isaiah 34:1-10 – Edom will be burned into pitch.

33. Isaiah 47:14 – Babylon to burn like stubble.

34. Isaiah 64:1-7, 10-11 – Zion to be burned into a waste place.

35. Isaiah 66:15-16, 24 – Zion to be judged by an unquenchable fire.

36. Jeremiah 4:4 – Jerusalem to be burned with fire that cannot be quenched.

37. Jeremiah 15:14 – Judah to be burned with the fire of God's anger (Babylon).

38. Jeremiah 17:1-4, 27 – Judah to be judged by fire for not keeping the law.

39. Jeremiah 21:10-14 – The King of Babylon shall burn Jerusalem with fire that none shall quench.

40. Jeremiah 34:2, 22 – Nebuchadnezzar shall burn Jerusalem with fire and make it uninhabited.

41. Jeremiah 37:8, 10 – Jerusalem will be judged by fire.

42. Jeremiah 38:17, 18, 23 – Jerusalem will be judged by fire (Babylon).

43. Jeremiah 43:12-13 – Egypt and her gods will be judged by fire (Babylon).

44. Jeremiah 48:45 – A fire from Heshbon and Sihon has destroyed Moab.

45. Jeremiah 50:32 – Babylon judged by fire because of pride.

46. Jeremiah 51:58 – Babylon and all nations gathered for the fire.

47. Jeremiah 52:13 – Nebuzaradan burned the house of Jehovah.

48. Lamentations 2:3-4 – God poured out his fire of wrath and burned up Jacob.

49. Lamentations 4:11 – God poured out his fire of wrath and destroyed Zion's foundations.

50. Ezekiel 5:4 – The House of Israel to be cast into the fire.

51. Ezekiel 15:1-8 – God's unprofitable vineyard to be burned up.

52. Ezekiel 10:2 – Coals of fire from God's throne cast upon Jerusalem.

53. Ezekiel 19:10-14 – God's unfruitful branches burned up.

54. Ezekiel 20:45-49 – The Forest of the South (Judah) to be burned up.

55. Ezekiel 21:28-32 – Ammon will be delivered into the fire of brutish men.

56. Ezekiel 22:17-22 – Israel's dross to be burned away by fire.

57. Ezekiel 23:25 – The residue (remnant) of Samaria and Jerusalem will be destroyed by fire.

58. Ezekiel 24:9-14 – Jerusalem to be judged by fire (Babylon).

59. Ezekiel 28:18-19 – Tyre forever overthrown by fire.

60. Ezekiel 30:6-9, 14, 16 – Egypt and all her cities to be judged by fire.

61. Ezekiel 36:5-7 – Edom and the residue of the nation burned with the fire of God's jealousy.

62. Ezekiel 38:17-23 – Gog from the land of Magog to be judged by fire, brimstone and smoke.

63. Ezekiel 39:6 – Magog and the isles will be burned by fire.

64. Daniel 7:9-12 – A fiery stream issues from God's throne.

65. Hosea 8:14 – God will send a fire upon Israel and Judah (Sennacherib).

66. Joel 1:19-20 – The fire has devoured the pastures (locusts).

67. Joel 2:3, 5 – Locusts are likened unto fire of judgment.

68. Joel 2:30 – Fire and pillars of smoke present in the Day of Judgment.

69. Amos 1:4, 7, 10, 12, 14; 2:2, 5 – God kindled a fire (brought judgment) on Hazael (Syria), Gaza (Philistia), Tyre (Phoenicia), Teman (Edom), Rabbah (Ammon), Moab, Judah.

70. Amos 5:6 – An unquenchable fire will destroy Joseph (Israel) at Bethel.

71. Obadiah 18 – Judah and Israel will burn among the stubble of Edom and none will remain.
72. Micah 1:2-7 – God will melt Israel and Judah.
73. Nahum 1:5-6 – God poured out his wrath like fire upon Nineveh.
74. Nahum 3:13-15 – God's fire devoured Nineveh's bars and people.
75. Habakkuk 2:13 – For Babylon's labor they will receive the fire of judgment.
76. Zephaniah 1:14-18 – Judah will be brought to a terrible end by the fire of Jehovah's judgment and nothing will be able to deliver them.
77. Zephaniah 3:8 – All of the nations of the earth will be devoured by the fire of Jehovah's jealousy.
78. Zechariah 2:5-13 – The fire of Jehovah's jealousy will protect his people.
79. Zechariah 3:2 – Judah is a brand plucked out of the fire.
80. Zechariah 9:4 – Tyre will be devoured with fire.
81. Zechariah 11:1-3 – The Cedars of Lebanon are devoured by fire.
82. Zechariah 12:6 – Judah will devour all of its enemies like fire devours wood.
83. Zechariah 13:9 – God will purify the nation of Judah by fire.
84. Malachi 3:1-6 – Jesus will cleanse the dross and purify the silver with fire.
85. Malachi 4:1-6 – Jesus will judge the proud wicked ones in the day of Jehovah by fire and will save the righteous.

APPENDIX ON "POURED OUT OR FORTH"

I.   Definition of the two words under consideration:

(1) ἐκχέω   (2) Ἐκχύνω

Thayer states that the meaning of these two words is identical, page 201.

A.   "To pour out, b. Metaph, to bestow or distribute largely. The Passive, is used of those who give themselves up to a thing, rush headlong into it."

B.   "To pour out, to shed as blood, to gush out, to spill, splatter; Methap. to give largely, bestow liberally; pass. to rush headlong into anything, be abandoned to" Bagster.

C.   Liddell-Scott on page 526-527.

1.   Pour out, pour away, hence spill a vessel; to be drained.

2.   Of words – pour forth, utter.

3.   Pour forth like water, squander, waste.

4.   Spread out.

5.   Throw down.

6.   Shed, shake off.

7.   Passively – to stream out or forth.

8.   Metaph. to be cast away or forgotten.

9.   Give oneself over to any emotion, to be overjoyed.

10. Poured forth, unconfined.

D.   In everyone of these the idea is that of unlimited outpouring.

II   The Parsing of "hath poured forth" in Acts 2:33. Third Person, Singular Number, First Aorist Tense, Indicative Mood, Active Voice.

A.   Third Person – The subject is being spoken of.

B.   Singular Number – Only one is under consideration.

C.   First Aorist –

"The function of the aorist there is a matter of tremendous importance. The *time of* action is past. The *kind* of action is punctiliar." Summers.

"The aorist these expresses action in its simplest form, undefined; it does not distinguish between complete or incomplete action. The aorist treats the action as a point . . . But time is expressed by the augment-punctiliar action in past time, generally.

In narrative the difference between the aorist indicative and the imperfect indicative is just this: the aorist indicative expresses punctiliar action in past time, while the imperfect indicative expresses durative action in past time" David.

D.   Indicative – the action is real, not potential.

E.   Active – the subject is doing the acting.

III. Grammatical Exegesis of Acts 2:33

Jesus poured out upon all flesh (vs. 16-17) the Holy Spirit in one point of time in the past by the time of Acts 2:33.

IV   Application of this Exegesis.

Thus Jesus' action was a one-time, point action in the past by the time of Acts 2:33.

V.   Comparison with other passages having the same construction.

A.   John 2:15 – At one time and point in the past Jesus poured out the money-changers' money (all of it).

B. Titus 3:6 – At one time and point in the past the Spirit was poured out for Paul and Titus (and all men, Acts 2:33, 39). (All of the Spirt was poured out.)

C. Revelation 16:1-4, 8, 10, 12, 17 – At one time and point the bowls of wrath (all that they contained) were poured out upon Rome bringing about its total destruction.

VI. The parsing of "was poured out" in Acts 10:45. Third Person, Singular Number, Perfect Tense, Indicative Mood, Passive Voice.

A. Third Person – The Subject is being spoken of.

B. Singular Number – Only one is under consideration.

C. Perfect Tense –

1. This is the Greek tense of "completed action" i.e., it indicates a completed action resulting in a state of being. The primary emphasis is on the resulting state of being. Involved in the Greek perfect are three ideas: an action in *progress,* its coming to a point of *culmination,* its existing as a *completed result.* Ray Summers.

2. The tense in Greek called perfect is really a present perfect. The perfect presents the action of the verb in a completed state or condition . . . The perfect expresses the continuance of completed action. It is then a combination of punctiliar and durative action . . . The perfect indicative generally expresses the present result of a past action . . . (examples) *gegrapha – I* wrote and the statement is still on record. *elalutha – I* came (punctiliar) and am still here (durative). Davis.

D. Indicative – The action is real, not potential.

E. Passive – Subject is being acted upon, not acting.

VII. Grammatical Exegesis of Acts 10:45.

The Holy Spirit had in the past been poured out (punctiliar, Acts 2:33) and was still present and available (durative) for the Gentiles. This was proven by the tongue-speaking going on (v. 46; Cf. 1 Corinthians 14:22).

VIII. Application of this Exegesis.

Thus Acts 2:17-39 teaches that the outpouring of the Holy Spirit was a promise for all men. Thus Acts twice (2:38 and 10:45) says God gave the Holy Spirit for all men. So Peter wants to know how could he withstand God in not being the baptizer so they might receive what God had promised and given–the Holy Spirit.

IX Comparison with other passages having the same construction. Only one, Romans 5:5. The love of God had in the past been shed abroad in their hearts and was still abiding there and having the result of giving them hope.

X. A listing of every time these words are found in New Testament.

1.   Matthew 9:17 – *Spilled* wine from old wineskins.

2.   Matthew 23:35 – *Shed* righteous blood.

3.   Matthew 26:28 – *Poured out* Jesus' Blood.

4.   Mark 14:24 – Ditto.

5.   Luke 5:37 – *Spilled* wine from old wineskins.

6.   Luke 11:50 – *Shed* prophet's blood.

7.   Luke 22:20 – *Poured out* Jesus' blood.

8.   John 2:15 – *Poured out* money-changers' money.

9.   Acts 1:18 – *Gushed out* – Judas' bowels.

10. Acts 2:17-18 – *Poured out* Holy Spirit.

11. Acts 2:33 – *Poured forth* what you see and hear (Holy Spirit).

12. Acts 10:45 – *Poured out* – the gift of the Holy Spirit.

13. Acts 22:20 – *Shed* Stephen's blood.

14. Rom. 3:15 – *Shed* martyr's blood.

15. Rom. 5:5 – *Shed abroad* . . . Love of God.

16. Titus 3:6 – *Poured out* . . . Holy Spirit.

17. Jude 11 (Margin) – Gave
    themselves away through Error of
    Balaam
    Ran riotously in   for hire.

18. Revelation 16:1-4, 8, 10, 12, 17 – *Poured out* Bowls
    of Wrath.

19. Revelation 16:6 – *Poured out* saints' blood.

IN ALL OF THESE THE IDEA IS A TOTAL, COMPLETE, ABSOLUTE, UNLIMITED OPERATION!!!

APPENDIX ON THE HOLY SPIRIT PASSAGES

1.	Genesis 1:2. In creation the Spirit is said to be moving, brooding, trembling as with anxiety or love over the chaos. This probably indicates His desire to bring order out of chaos.

2.	Genesis 6:3. God said His Spirit would cease to strive with man for his obedience, and He (God) would destroy them with a flood. The Spirit was striving through the preachings of Noah (1 Peter 3:18-21).

3.	Genesis 41:38. Because of his power to interpret dreams, Pharaoh recognizes in Joseph the Spirit of God. The Spirit is then the Revealer of dreams in the Old Testament.

4.	Exodus 31:3. Because of their long slavery causing a lack of skilled workers, God's Spirit gave some men the skill to be artisans and builders.

5.	Exodus 35:31. Same as above.

6.	Numbers 11:27, 25, 26, 29. The Spirit of God that rested upon Moses was placed upon the seventy elders to empower them in judgment. Two of them went out and prophesied and Moses said he wished God's Spirit could rest upon all that they might be prophets. God's Spirit is the Spirit of the Prophets.

7.	Numbers 24:2. Balaam gave his message by the power of the Holy Spirit.

8.	Numbers 27:1. Joshua, Moses' successor, had the Spirit in him.

9.   Judges 3:10. The Spirit of Jehovah came upon Othniel, the first judge, and he went to battle. The Spirit of God empowers God's generals.

10.   Judges 6:34. The same as above in the case of Gideon.

11.   Judges 11:29. The same as above in the case of Jephthah.

12.   Judges 13:25; 14:6, 19; 15:14. The Spirit of Jehovah came repeatedly upon Samson and was the secret of his great strength.

13.   1 Samuel 10:6, 10; 11:6. The Spirit of Jehovah came upon Saul, empowering him to be king.

14.   1 Samuel 16:13. The Spirit begins to move David, God's new king, from this day forward.

15.   1 Samuel 16:14. The Spirit of Jehovah departs from Saul and an evil spirit from Jehovah takes its place.

16.   1 Samuel 19:20, 23. To allow David to escape from Saul, the Spirit of Jehovah comes upon Saul and he prophesied. This shows that the Spirit can even empower a wicked man to prophesy.

17.   2 Samuel 23:2. The Spirit of God spake by David.

18.   1 Kings 18:12. Obadiah said the Spirit of Jehovah could carry Elijah to some safe place away from Ahab and Jezebel.

19.   1 Kings 22:24. Zedekiah thought he was led by the Spirit of Jehovah. Micah said he would find out when he was running from the Syrians. Also 2 Chronicles 18:23.

20.   2 Kings 2:16. Some thought the Spirit had cast Elijah upon some mountain or into some valley.

21.   1 Chronicles 12:18. The Spirit of Jehovah came upon Amasai, one of David's mighty men

22. 1 Chronicles 28:12. The Holy Spirit gave David and David gave to Solomon the pattern for the temple.

23. 2 Chronicles 15:1. The Spirit of Jehovah came upon Azariah, a prophet.

24. 2 Chronicles 20:14. The Spirit of Jehovah came upon Jahaziel, a Levite and he prophesied.

25. Nehemiah 9:20. God gave Israel His good Spirit to instruct them.

26. 2 Chronicles 24:20. The Spirit of God came upon Zechariah, a priest, and he prophesied.

27. Nehemiah 9:30. God had testified against Israel by His Spirit through the prophets.

28. Job 26:13. God's Spirit garnished the heavens, according to Bildad.

29. Job 33:4. Elihu claims to be made by the Spirit – a claim to inspiration.

30. Psalms 51:11. David pleads that God will not take His Spirit from him.

31. Psalms 104:30. The world was created and renewed by God's Spirit.

32. Psalms 139:7. There is no place in heaven or on earth or under the earth where one could escape from God's Spirit. The Spirit of God is omnipresent.

33. Psalms 143:10. David asks God's Spirit to lead him (margin reading).

34. Isaiah 11:2. God's Spirit to rest upon God's Branch (Christ).

35. Isaiah 30:1. Israel does not take counsel of God's Spirit (through Isaiah).

36. Isaiah 32:15. Israel will become fruitful again when God's Spirit is poured out upon them.

37. Isaiah 34:16. Edom will be altogether possessed by Israel by the gathering of God's Spirit. God's Spirit works providentially in destroying and preserving nations.

38. Isaiah 40:13. Nobody is the Spirit's instructor.

39. Isaiah 42:1. God's Spirit to be put upon God's chosen one (Christ, cf. Luke 4:16ff).

40. Isaiah 44:3. God's Spirit to be poured out upon Israel's seed.

41. Isaiah 48:16. Jehovah and His Spirit had sent Isaiah to preach.

42. Isaiah 59:19. The Spirit of Jehovah will raise up a standard and stop the march of God's enemies (marginal reading).

43. Isaiah 59:21. God's Spirit is upon Isaiah and will not depart.

44. Isaiah 61:1. The Spirit of Jehovah will be upon Jesus (Cf. Luke 4:16ff).

45. Isaiah 63:10. Israel rebelled and grieved God's Spirit.

46. Isaiah 63:11. God placed His Holy Spirit in the midst of Israel.

47. Isaiah 63:14. God's Spirit led Israel in the wilderness and caused them to rest in the promised land (through Moses and Joshua and the Elders).

48. Ezekiel 2:2. The Spirit entered into Ezekiel.

49. Ezekiel 3:12, 14. The Spirit lifted up Ezekiel and carried him away.

50. Ezekiel 3:24. The Spirit entered Ezekiel.

51. Ezekiel 8:3. The Spirit lifted him up.

52. Ezekiel 11:1. Same as above.

53. Ezekiel 11:5. The Spirit fell upon Ezekiel.

54. Ezekiel 11:24. The Spirit lifted him up and God carried him in a vision by the Spirit of God.

55. Ezekiel 36:27. God is going to put His Spirit in redeemed Israel.

56. Ezekiel 37:1. God carried Ezekiel by the Spirit into the valley of bones.

57. Ezekiel 37:14. God will put His Spirit in redeemed Israel.

58. Ezekiel 39:29. God will pour out His Spirit upon redeemed Israel.

59. Ezekiel 43:5. The Spirit picked him up and carried him to the temple.

60. Daniel 4:8, 9, 18. Nebuchadnezzar believes the Spirit of the Holy God (or gods) dwells in Daniel.

61. Daniel 5:11. Belshazzar's wife believes the Spirit dwells in Daniel.

62. Joel 2:28-29. God will pour out His Spirit upon all flesh-sons, daughters, servants and handmaids.

63. Micah 2:7. The Spirit of Jehovah cannot be straitened, put into difficulty.

64. Micah 3:8. The Spirit was the secret of Micah's power.

65. Haggai 2:5. God's Spirit abode among Israel when they came out of Egypt.

66. Zechariah 4:6. The temple will be completed by the power of God's Spirit.

67.   Zechariah 6:8. God's Spirit has been satisfied by the judgment in the North.

68.   Zechariah 7:12. God's Spirit had been in the former prophets.

69.   Malachi 2:15. No one who had even the residue of God's Spirit had put away his wife.

70.   Matthew 1:18, 20. Jesus will be begotten in the womb through the Holy Spirit.

71.   Matthew 3:11. Jesus is the only one able to baptize in the Holy Spirit.

72.   Matthew 3:16. The Holy Spirit descends upon Jesus at his baptism.

73.   Matthew 4:1. The Spirit leads Jesus into the wilderness of temptation.

74.   Matthew 10:20. The Holy Spirit will give the apostles the "how" and the "what" to say when persecuted and tried.

75.   Matthew 12:18. Jesus is the fulfillment of Isaiah 42:1ff which states that the Spirit would be upon the Lord's chosen one.

76.   Matthew 12:28. Jesus performed his miracles by the power of the Holy Spirit.

77.   Matthew 12:31, 32. The blasphemy of the Holy Spirit.

78.   Matthew 22:43. David in the Spirit called Jesus Lord in Psalms 110.

79.   Matthew 28:19. Baptism is in the name of the Father and of the Son and of the Holy Spirit.

80.   Mark 1:8. Jesus to baptize in the Spirit.

81.   Mark 1:10. Spirit descends upon Jesus at his baptism.

82. Mark 1:12. The Spirit drives Jesus forth into the wilderness of temptation.

83. Mark 3:29. The blasphemy against the Holy Spirit.

84. Mark 12:36. David in the Spirit called Jesus Lord in Psalms 110.

85. Mark 13:11. The apostles will be given by the Spirit what to speak.

86. Luke 1:15. John the Baptist to be filled with the Spirit from his mother's womb.

87. Luke 1:35. The power in Jesus' virgin birth is the Holy Spirit.

88. Luke 1:41. Elisabeth, John the Baptist's mother, is filled with the Holy Spirit.

89. Luke 1:67. Zacharias, John the Baptist's father, is filled with the Holy Spirit.

90. Luke 2:25. The Spirit is upon Simeon.

91. Luke 2:26. The Spirit revealed to him that he would see the Messiah.

92. Luke 2:27. He came in the Spirit into the temple and saw Jesus.

93. Luke 3:16. Jesus is the only one who will baptize in the Holy Spirit.

94. Luke 3:22. The Spirit descends upon Jesus at his baptism.

95. Luke 4:1. Jesus is led of the Spirit in the wilderness for forty days.

96. Luke 4:14. Jesus returned in the power of the Spirit into Galilee.

97. Luke 4:18. The Spirit of the Lord had anointed Jesus for his ministry.

98. Luke 10:21. Jesus rejoiced in the Spirit at the return of the seventy.

99. Luke 11:13. God gives the Holy Spirit to them that ask Him.

100. Luke 12:10. The blasphemy against the Holy Spirit.

101. Luke 12:12. The Holy Spirit will teach the apostles what to say.

102. John 1:32. John beheld the Spirit descend as a dove upon Jesus at baptism.

103. John 1:33. Jesus is the one who will baptize in the Holy Spirit.

104. John 3:5, 6, 8. The Spirit is indispensable in the New Birth.

105. John 3:34. Jesus continues to give the Spirit not by measure.

106. John 7:39. After Jesus' glorification the Spirit was to reside within the believers.

107. John 14:17. The Spirit had been with the apostles but now to be in them.

108. John 14:26. The Spirit to teach the apostles all things and bring all that Jesus has said to remembrance.

109. John 15:26. The Spirit is to bear witness to Jesus.

110. John 16:13. The Spirit is to guide them into all the truth and declare the things that are to come.

111. John 20:22. "Receive ye the Holy Spirit."

112. Acts 1:2. The commandments Jesus gave the apostles between resurrection and ascension were through the Holy Spirit.

113. Acts 1:5. They were to be baptized with the Holy Spirit not many days hence.

114. Acts 1:8. They were to receive power after the Holy Spirit was come.

115. Acts 1:16. The Holy Spirit spoke through the mouth of David.

116. Acts 2:4. The apostles were filled with the Holy Spirit and spoke as the Spirit gave them utterance.

117. Acts 2:17, 18. The Spirit had been poured out upon all flesh.

118. Acts 2:33. Jesus had poured out the promise of the Father, the Holy Spirit.

119. Acts 2:38. All those who repent and are baptized can receive the gift of the Holy Spirit.

120. Acts. 4:8. Peter, filled with the Holy Spirit, answers the Sanhedrin.

121. Acts 4:31. The whole church, after praying, are filled with the Holy Spirit and depart to preach with boldness.

122. Acts 5:3, 9. Ananias and Sapphira conspire together to lie unto and try the Holy Spirit of the Lord.

123. Acts. 5:32. The Spirit that God gives to the obedient is a witness to Jesus.

124. Acts 6:3, 5. The servants (deacons) of the Jerusalem church were to be men full of the Spirit.

125. Acts 6:10. The Libertines could not withstand the Holy Spirit by which Stephan spoke.

126. Acts 7:51. The Jews had through their history resisted the Holy Spirit who spoke in the prophets.

127. Acts 7:55. Stephan was full of the Holy Spirit.

128. Acts 8:15-19. The Holy Spirit fell upon the Samaritans (empowering them outwardly) through the laying on of the apostles' hands. Simon wanted to buy this power.

129. Acts 8:29. The Spirit told Philip to join himself to the chariot of the Eunuch.

130. Acts 8:39. The Spirit caught Philip away that the Eunuch saw him no more.

131. Acts 10:19. The Spirit told Peter to go with Cornelius' servants.

132. Acts 10:38. Jesus was anointed with the Holy Spirit and power.

133. Acts 10:44. The Holy Spirit fell on (empowering) Cornelius and the other Gentiles.

134. Acts 10:45. The Holy Spirit had in the past (Pentecost) been poured out for the Gentiles and was this day still available for them through faith's obedience.

135. Acts 10:47. The Gentiles had received the Spirit (directly from heaven) to empower them, just as the Samaritans had received the Spirit (through apostolic hands) to empower them; and just (directly from heaven) as the apostles had on Pentecost. Now who is going to forbid them to be baptized that they might become saved.

136. Acts 11:12. Peter said the Spirit bade him make no distinction between Jew and Gentile.

137. Acts 11:15. Peter said the Holy Spirit fell on the Gentiles as he had on the apostles in the beginning. "As" is an adverb of manner, not degree, in the Greek.

138. Acts 11:16. This "reminded" Peter that the Lord had promised a baptism in the Spirit which he had said on Pentecost was for all flesh.

139. Acts 11:24. Barnabas was a man full of the Holy Spirit.

140. Acts 11:28. Agabus signified by the Spirit that a famine was in the future.

141. Acts 13:2. The Holy Spirit told the prophets of Antioch to separate Saul and Barnabas.

142. Acts 13:4. Barnabas and Saul were sent forth by the Holy Spirit.

143. Acts 13:9. Paul, filled with the Spirit, smote Elymas blind for a season.

144. Acts 13:52. The disciples in Antioch of Pisidia are filled with joy and with the Holy Spirit.

145. Acts 15:8. God bear the Gentiles witness giving them the Holy Spirit.

146. Acts 15:28. It seemed good to the Holy Spirit and the apostles to not bind the law of Moses on the Gentiles.

147. Acts 16:6, 7. The Holy Spirit forbade and did not permit Paul and his company to go into Asia or Bithynia.

148. Acts 19:2. Those baptized by Apollos do not know about the gift of the Spirit received when one is baptized in the name of (by the authority of) Christ.

149. Acts 19:6. They receive the Spirit (metonymy signifying some gift) through the laying on of Paul's hands.

150. Acts 20:23. The Holy Spirit is testifying in every city that Paul will be bound in Jerusalem.

151. Acts 20:28. The Holy Spirit makes men elders, overseers of God's flock.

152. Acts 21:4. The disciples in Tyre said through the Spirit that Paul should not go to Jerusalem.

153. Acts 21:11. Agabus says the Holy Spirit said Paul would be bound in Jerusalem.

154. Acts 28:25. The Holy Spirit spake through Isaiah.

155. Romans 5:5. The Holy Spirit, God's gift, sheds love abroad in hearts.

156. Romans 8:2. Spirit makes me free from law of sin and death.

157. Romans 8:4. The Christian walks after the Spirit.

158. Romans 8:5. The Christian minds the things of the Spirit.

159. Romans 8:9a. The Christian is not in the flesh but in the Spirit.

160. Romans 8:9b. If do not have Spirit, do not belong to Christ.

161. Romans 8:11. The Spirit that dwells in us will resurrect our mortal bodies.

162. Romans 8:13. By the Spirit we put to death the deeds of the flesh.

163. Romans 8:14. Sons of God are led by the Spirit of God.

164. Romans 8:16. The Spirit is a co-witness with my spirit that I am son of God.

165. Romans 8:23. We have the first-fruits of the Spirit.

166. Romans 8:26-27. The Holy Spirit intercedes for the Christian in prayer.

167. Romans 9:1. Paul's conscience bears witness in the Spirit of his love for the Jew.

168. Romans 14:17. Kingdom is Righteousness, peace and joy in the Holy Spirit.

169. Romans 15:13. Abundant hope for the Christian in the power of the Holy Spirit.

170. Romans 15:16. Paul's ministry is sanctified by the Holy Spirit.

171. Romans 15:19. Wonders, signs in the power of the Holy Spirit.

172. Romans 15:30. Paul beseeches by the love of the Spirit.

173. 1 Corinthians 2:4. Demonstration of the Spirit and of power.

174. 1 Corinthians 2:10-12. The Spirit revealed the hidden things of God to the apostles.

175. 1 Corinthians 2:13. The apostles spoke the things of the Spirit in words of the Spirit. Revelation plus inspiration.

176. 1 Corinthians 2:14. The natural man cannot receive these things revealed and written by the Spirit.

177. 1 Corinthians 3:16. The church is a temple of the Holy Spirit.

178. 1 Corinthians 6:11. The Corinthians had been washed, sanctified and justified in the name of Christ and in the Spirit of our Lord.

179. 1 Corinthians 6:19. The body of the Christian is a temple of the Holy Spirit.

180. 1 Corinthians 7:40. Paul thinks he has the Spirit of God.

181. 1 Corinthians 12:3. No one by the Spirit curses Jesus and only by the Spirit can one say that He is Lord.

182. 1 Corinthians 12:4-11. The miraculous gifts are given and distributed by the One Spirit of God according to his sovereign will.

183. 1 Corinthians 12:13. By this one Spirit we are all baptized into one body. Either because it is through His instructions or because we are his representatives in baptizing those who we teach.

184. 1 Corinthians 14:2. The one who speaks in a tongue speaks mysteries in the Spirit.

185. 1 Corinthians 14:14, 15, 16. One can sing, pray, give thanks in a tongue in the Spirit but not to do so in the assembly unless can understand and edify the church by interpreting.

186. 2 Corinthians 1:22. We are established, sealed and given the earnest of the Spirit in our hearts.

187. 2 Corinthians 3:3. The Corinthians were Paul's epistles written by the Holy Spirit.

188. 2 Corinthians 3:17. The Spirit is Lord and where the Spirit is there is liberty.

189. 2 Corinthians 5:5. God has given us the earnest of the Spirit.

190. 2 Corinthians 6:6. One of the things that commended Paul was that he was "in the Holy Spirit."

191. 2 Corinthians 13:14. The communion, fellowship of the Spirit.

192. Galatians 3:2. The Galatians had received the Spirit through the hearing of faith.

193. Galatians 3:3. Their progress was through the Spirit.

194. Galatians 3:5. The present manifestations of the Spirit had been because of faith.

195. Galatians 3:14. They had received the promise of the Spirit through faith.

196. Galatians 4:6. Because we are sons God gives us His Spirit.

197. Galatians 4:29. We like Isaac are born after the Spirit.

198. Galatians 5:5. Through the Spirit we wait for the hope of righteousness.

199. Galatians 5:16. We are to walk after the Spirit.

200. Galatians 5:17. There is a warfare between the flesh and the Spirit.

201. Galatians 5:18. Being led by the Spirit frees me from the system of the law.

202. Galatians 5:22. The Spirit bears marvelous fruit in the Christian's life.

203. Galatians 5:25. We can march by the Spirit if we live by the Spirit.

204. Galatians 6:8. To sow unto the Spirit will enable us to reap of the Spirit eternal life.

205. Ephesians 1:13. The Spirit is the Christian's seal.

206. Ephesians 1:14. The Spirit is the earnest of our salvation.

207. Ephesians 2:18. The Spirit is the access to God.

208. Ephesians 2:22. God dwells in me through the Spirit.

209. Ephesians 3:5. The Spirit revealed the mystery to the apostles and prophets.

210. Ephesians 3:16. The Christian is strengthened in his inward man through the Spirit.

211. Ephesians 4:3. The unity of the church is the unity of the Spirit.

212. Ephesians 4:4. There is only one Spirit, the Holy Spirit.

213. Ephesians 4:30. We can grieve the Holy Spirit of God, our seal.

214. Ephesians 5:18. My worship will be controlled by my being filled with the Spirit.

215. Ephesians 6:17. The word of God is the sword of the Spirit.

216. Ephesians 6:18. Prayer should be in the Holy Spirit.

217. Philippians 1:19. The supply of the Spirit turns out to salvation.

218. Philippians 2:1. The fellowship of the Spirit.

219. Philippians 3:3. Worship by the Spirit of our God.

220. Colossians 1:8. The Colossians loved Paul in the Spirit.

221. 1 Thessalonians 1:5. The word of God came in power and in the Holy Spirit.

222. 1 Thessalonians 4:8. God gives His Spirit unto us.

223. 1 Thessalonians 1:6. They had received the word of God in much affliction with joy in the Holy Spirit.

224. 1 Thessalonians 5:19. Do not quench the Spirit (either through quenching the word or His power through that word).

225. 2 Thessalonians 2:13. They had been sanctified by the Holy Spirit.

226. 1 Timothy 3:16. Jesus was justified by the Spirit.

227. 1 Timothy 4:1. The Spirit foretold the apostasy.

228. 2 Timothy 1:14. Guard the deposit through the Holy Spirit which dwells in you.

229. Titus 3:5. Saved through the washing of regeneration and the renewing of the Holy Spirit.

230. Hebrews 2:4. The miracles of the Holy Spirit confirmed the spoken word of the apostles.

231. Hebrews 3:7. The Holy Spirit spoke in Psalms 95.

232. Hebrews 6:4. Christians are partakers of the Holy Spirit.

233. Hebrews 9:8. The Holy Spirit thus signifying (i.e. by the types of the Old Testament).

234. Hebrews 9:14. Jesus offered Himself without blemish through the power of the Holy Spirit.

235. Hebrews 10:15. The Holy Spirit beareth witness in Jeremiah 31.

236. Hebrews 10:29. Those who return to their former life do despite unto the Spirit.

237. James 4:5. The Spirit which dwells in us yearns for our obedience with a jealous attitude.

238. 1 Peter 1:2. The Sanctification of the Spirit.

239. 1 Peter 1:11. The Spirit of Christ was in the prophets.

240. 1 Peter 1:12. Those who preach the gospel do so by the Holy Spirit sent forth from heaven.

241. 1 Peter 3:18. Jesus was raised by the same Spirit that preached through Noah, the Holy Spirit.

242. 1 Peter 4:14. When we're reproached for the name of Christ the spirit of glory and the Spirit of God resteth upon us.

243. 2 Peter 1:21. All the holy men of God spake as they were moved by the Holy Spirit.

244. 1 John 3:24; 4:13. We know that we are in God and He in us by the Spirit that He has given us.

245. 1 John 4:2. Those who have the Spirit of God preach that Jesus came in the flesh.

246. 1 John 5:7. The Spirit bears witness in truth.

247. 1 John 5:8. The Spirit bears witness with the water and the blood.

248. Jude 19. Those who are carnal and make divisions do not have the Spirit.

249. Jude 20. We need to be praying in the Spirit in order to be matured.

250. Revelation 1:4. John sends greetings from the Seven Spirits (the Holy Spirit).

251. Revelation 1:10. John is in the Spirit (under His control) on the Lord's day.

252. Revelation 2:7, 11, 17, 39; 3:1, 6, 13, 22. The Spirit speaks to the churches.

253. Revelation 4:2. John is in the Spirit.

254. Revelation 4:5. The Seven Spirits are before the throne of God.

255. Revelation 5:6. The seven Spirits are sent throughout the earth.

256. Revelation 14:13. The Spirit says the dead saints are blessed.

257. Revelation 17:3. The Spirit carries John away into the wilderness to see the harlot.

258. Revelation 21:10. John is carried away in the Spirit unto a high mountain.

259. Revelation 22:17. The Spirit has one last word to say as he closes his book: Come to Christ. The Spirit's last invitation.

APPENDIX ON THE HOLY SPIRIT
AND THE RESTORATION MOVEMENT

This section should not be construed as an appeal to these great men as authorities. However, even historically speaking, this section should be of great value to the earnest seekers of truth. Many of the men here quoted were great scholars as well as humble New Testament Christians. It is interesting to see what the mainstream of the church for the past 150 years have believed concerning the Holy Spirit.

ALEXANDER CAMPBELL. In 1823, Campbell began his paper, The *Christian Baptist*. In Volume II, August 2, 1824, in a work called *Essays on the work of the Holy Spirit in the Salvation of Men – No. V.*, Campbell says,

> Hitherto we have been considering the Holy Spirit as the Spirit of Wisdom, and the Spirit of Power. We have not yet introduced him as the Spirit of Holiness or of Goodness. This will be more particularly attended to by and by – For it not only revealed as the Spirit of wisdom and power, but also as the Spirit of all goodness in man. As the Spirit of Wisdom and of Power, it was the author of all the miraculous, spiritual gifts, and prophecy; but as the Spirit of Goodness, it is the author of that principle in Christians, which inclines and enables them to cry, Abba, Father.

On the March 7, 1825 issue, Campbell, discussing the doctrine of "Direct Operation," says:

> And how much happier would be the majority of Christians, if instead of eagerly contending about

the fashionable theories of religion, they would remember that every good and perfect gift comes down from the Father of Lights – that he has promised his Holy Spirit to them that ask him, and that every necessary blessing is bestowed upon all them who, believing that God is a rewarder of them that diligently seek him, ask for those favors comprised in – the love of God, the grace of the Lord Jesus Christ, and the fellowship of the Holy Spirit.

In the July 7, 1828 Issue, Campbell discusses Christian Immersion in an article entitled *Ancient Gospel – No. VII*. Near the end of that essay he says:

For so soon as any person, through faith and immersion, is adopted into the family of God, and becomes one of the sons of God, then he receives the Spirit of Christ: for as says Paul, "Because you are sons, God has sent forth the Spirit of His Son into your hearts, causing you to cry Abba, Father." This is the Holy Spirit, which all who are now immersed through faith in Christ's blood for the remission of sins, receive, as we explained in our fifth essay on this subject. It is in this sense only that the phrase "gift of the Holy Spirit" can now be understood ... How gracious this institution! It give to the convert a sensible pledge that God, through the blood of Christ, has washed away his sins, has adopted him into His family, and made him an heir of all things through Christ. Thus, according to the tenner of the New Testament, God dwells in him and he in God by the Spirit imparted to him. Thus he is constituted a Christian or a disciple of Jesus Christ.

In the ninth essay on the Ancient Gospel in the October 6, 1828 Issue, Campbell sums up:

> In the natural order of the evangelical economy, the items stand thus; – 1. Faith; 2. Reformation; 3. Immersion; 4. Remission of Sins; 5. Holy Spirit; 6. Eternal life ... Remission of sins as inseparably accompanies immersion, as reformation accompanies faith. Then the Holy Spirit is bestowed, and the disciple is filled with the spirit of adoption, which inspires him with filial confidence in God ... Those who proclaim faith in the Lord Jesus Christ and reformation in order to immersion; and immersion in order to forgiveness and the Holy Spirit, proclaim the same gospel which the apostles proclaimed ... The inward repentance and the outward reformation, which are coetaneous, are first constitutionally exhibited in the act of immersion into the name of the Lord Jesus for the remission of sins. The old sins are thus purified through faith in the blood of the Messiah, according to the divine appointment. The Holy Spirit is then given, for Jesus Christ is now glorified in heaven and upon earth.

In 1834 in the _Millennial Harbinger_ Campbell wrote:

> The phrase, "the gift of the Holy Spirit," means the Holy Spirit himself given, as foretold by Joel, and vouchsafed to Jews and Gentiles at the erection of the kingdom of the Messiah, and on their

admission into it ... Be it observed that the Holy
Spirit himself is a *gift*. He is not the donor but the
donation ... For it is evident that the Spirit himself,
though a gift, displayed his presence in the spiritual
men by such measures or distributions of his power
as seemed good to himself. Hear Paul in 1
Corinthians 12:9-10 ... These are spiritual gifts,
portion, measures of the Spirit, bestowed by
himself on those to whom he was given.

In the *Millennial Harbinger* for 1854 we read the
following in an article explaining the restorers' plea:

"That is to say, upon a sincere belief of the
testimony borne by prophets and apostles,
respecting the birth, the life, the character, the
death, resurrection, and ascension of Christ,
accompanied by a true repentance, the sinner is to
be immersed for the remission of sins, and the
reception of the Holy Spirit, and is then to be
added to the church, to walk in the commandments
of the Lord, and manifest the graces of Christian
character. If, then, they have any theory of
conversion, it is simply that of the natural order of
cause and effect; the Holy Spirit, through the
divine testimony, being conceived to produce the
faith of the gospel; this faith leading to repentance,
to reformation, and consequent obedience to the
commands of the gospel; and this obedience
securing the immediate enjoyment of its promised
blessings, the pardon of sins, and the indwelling of
the Holy Spirit. The possession of the Holy Spirit
is regarded as the evidence"of Sonship to God, and

as the earnest of the spiritual and glorious inheritance promised to the righteous ... And with respect to the Holy Spirit, they (the Christians in that day, RR) believe that he is the 'Spirit of God' the 'Comforter,' the 'Spirit of Christ,' who spoke by the prophets and apostles, filling them with divine wisdom and power; and that he is "the gift of God," by whose presence they are rendered' temples of the living God,' and 'sanctified,' 'renewed,' and saved."

Robert Richardson, Campbell's son-in-law, biographer, and editor of the *Millennial Harbinger*, wrote in 1852 the following:

"The chief cause of misapprehension in regard to the subject of Spiritual influence, is, as it appears to me, to be found in the fact, that most persons confound the agency of the Spirit in *conversion,* with the influence he exerts as *indwelling in the heart of the believer. . .* We regard, however, the conversion of the sinner and the sanctification of the believer, as distinct matters, accomplished, indeed, by the same Spirit, but in a different manner, and from a widely different position. We conceive the Holy Spirit to stand to the sinner in a relation very distinct from that in which he stands to him who is a member of the family of God. With the former, he is an outward witness for the truth; but the latter "has the witness *in himself.* " (I believe he missed this point, R R). To the first he is an unknown visitant or stranger; to the last, he is an indwelling and cherished guest. To the sinner,

he is as the rain which falls upon the surface of the
earth; to the believer, he is as a fountain *from
within,* springing up into everlasting life. . . That
which is pure, must be received into a pure vessel;
and it is not until the heart is "purified by faith,"
that the Holy Spirit may enter to dwell therein.
This is the view everywhere given in the
Scriptures. Peter said to the believing penitents on
the day of Pentecost, "Reform and be baptized for
the remission of sins, and you shall (then) receive
the gift of the Holy Spirit." Paul wrote to the
Ephesians, "In Christ ye also trusted, after ye heard
the word of truth, the gospel of your salvation, in
whom also, *after that ye believed,* ye were sealed
with the Holy Spirit of promise, which is an
earnest of our inheritance."

And also to the Galatians: *"Because ye are sons,*
God hath sent forth the Spirit of his Son into your
hearts, crying Abba, Father." It is, on the other
hand, nowhere stated that the Holy Spirit was
given to any one to make him a believer, or a child
of God. . . Being thus born from above, he is
prepared to *receive* that Spirit of adoption, that
Holy Spirit or Comforter, which God bestows upon
all his children, and which becomes to them an
internal indwelling witness, and an earnest of their
eternal inheritance, and produces in them, through
its sanctifying influences and those of the truth it
has revealed, the precious fruits of love, joy, peace
and righteousness.

In 1835 Campbell wrote *The Christian System* in an attempt to explain fully the principles of New Testament Christianity. Several quotes from this work are especially revealing in regard to Campbell's concept to the Spirit and his work.

> The Spirit is said to do, and to have done, all that God does and all that God has done. . . Anciently, or before time; it was God, the Word of God, and the Spirit of God. But now, in the development of the Christian scheme, it is "the Father, the Son, and the Holy Spirit." – one God, even the Father, and one Lord Jesus Christ, even the Savior; and one Spirit, even the Advocate, the Sanctifier, and the Comforter of Christ's body–the church. Jesus is the *head,* and the Spirit is the *life* and animating principle of that body, page 24.

> We also have believed all this (concerning the Christ), repented of our sins, and been immersed into Christ. We have assumed him as our Leader, our Prophet, Priest, and King; and put ourselves under his guidance. Having disowned the great apostate and his ranks, and enlisted under the Messiah, and taken sides with the Lord's Anointed, he now proposes to put his Holy Spirit within us, to furnish us for the good fight of faith, and to anoint us as the sons and heirs of God ... As observed in its proper place, the Spirit of God is the perfecter and finisher of all divine works. . . The Spirit of God inspired all the spiritual ideas in the New Testament, and confirmed them by miracles; and he is ever present with the word that

he inspired. He descended from heaven on the day
of Pentecost, and has not formally ascended since.
In the sense in which he descended he certainly has
not ascended; for he is animate and inspired with
new life the church or temple of the Lord. . . Now
we cannot separate the Spirit and the word of God,
and ascribe so much power to the one and so much
to the other; for so did not the apostles. Whatever
the word does, the Spirit does; and whatever the
Spirit does in converting men, the word does. We
neither believe nor teach abstract Spirit nor
abstract word, but word and Spirit, Spirit and
word, pages 63 and 64.

The Holy Spirit is, then, the author of all our
holiness; and in the struggle after victory over sin
and temptation, "it helps our infirmities," and
comforts us seasonably bringing to our
remembrance the promises of Christ, and
"strengthens us with all might, in the new and
inner man." And thus "God works in us to will and
to do of his own benevolence," "while we are
working out our own salvation with fear and
trembling." Christians are, therefore, clearly and
unequivocally temples of the Holy Spirit; and they
are quickened, animated, encouraged, and
sanctified by the power and influence of the Spirit
God, working in them through the truth. . . To
those, then, who believe, repent, and obey the
gospel, he actually communicates of his Good
Spirit. The fruits of that Spirit in them are "love,
joy, peace, longsuffering, gentleness, goodness,

Gal. 5:22

fidelity, meekness, temperance." The attributes of character which distinguish the new man are each of them communications of the Holy Spirit, and thus are we the sons of God in fact, as well as in title, under the dispensation of the Holy Spirit, page 66.

All who "believe in him are justified from all things;" because this faith is living, active, operative, and perfected by "obeying from the heart that form of doctrine delivered to us." Hence such persons repent of their sins and obey the gospel. They receive the Holy Spirit of God and the promise of eternal life–walk in the Spirit, and are sanctified to God, and constituted heirs of God and joint heirs with Christ. They shall be raised from the dead incorruptible, immortal, and shall live forever with the Lord; while those "who know not God, and obey not the gospel of his Son, shall perish with an everlasting destruction from the presence of the Lord and from the glory of his power," page 72.

But it is in the person and mission of the INCARNATE WORD that we learn that *God is Love.* That God gave his Son for us, and yet gives his Spirit to us – and thus gives us himself – are the mysterious and transcendent proofs of the most August proposition in the universe. The gospel, Heaven's wisdom and power combined, God's own expedient for the renovation of human nature, is neither more nor less than the illustration and proof of this regenerating proposition, page 254.

RENEWING OF THE HOLY SPIRIT. "He has saved us," says the Apostle Paul, "by the bath of regeneration and the *renewing of the Holy Spirit,* which he poured on us richly through Jesus Christ our Savior; that, being justified by his favor (in the bath of regeneration) we might be made heirs according to the hope of eternal life.'; Thus, and not by works of righteousness, he has saved us. Consequently, being born of water and the renewing of the Holy Spirit are not works of merit or righteousness, but only the means of enjoyment. But this pouring out of the influences, this renewing of the Holy Spirit, is as necessary as the bath of regeneration to the salvation of the soul, and to the enjoyment of the hope of heaven, of which the apostle speaks. In the kingdom' into which we are born of water, the Holy Spirit is as the atmosphere in the kingdom of nature; we mean that the influences of the Holy Spirit are as necessary to *the new life,* as the atmosphere is to our animal life in the kingdom of nature. All that is done in us before regeneration, God our Father effects by *the word,* or the gospel as dictated and confirmed by his Holy Spirit. But after we are thus begotten and born by the Spirit of God–the Holy Spirit is shed on us richly through Jesus Christ our Savior; of which the peace of mind, the love, the joy, and the hope of the regenerate is full proof; for those are among the fruits of that Holy Spirit of promise of which we speak. Thus commences the new life, page 267.

Great as the opposition is to truth and salvation, we have no reason to despond. Greater are our friends and allies, and infinitely more powerful, than all our cnemics. God is on our side-Jesus Christ is our King – the Holy Spirit is at our disposal–angels are his ministering servants – the prayers of all the prophets, apostles, saints, and martyrs are for our success – our brethren are numerous and strong – they have the sword of the Spirit, the shield of faith, the helmet of Salvation, the breastplate of righteousness, the artillery of truth, the arguments of God, the preparation of the gospel of peace – our Commander and Captain is the most successful General that ever entered the field of war – he never lost a battle – he is wonderful in council, excellent in working, valiant in fight – the Lord of *hosts* is his name . . . If a Roman could say, "Nothing is to be feared under the auspices of Caesar," may not the Christian say, "There is no despair under the guardianship of Messiah the King," page 337.

If the Spirit of the Lord was necessary to the success of Gideon and Warak, and Samson and David, and all the great warriors of Israel according to the flesh, who fought the battles of the Lord with the sword, the sling, and the bow; who can say that it is not necessary to those who draw the Sword of the Spirit and fight the good fight of faith? In my judgment it is as necessary now as then – necessary, I mean to equal success necessary to the success of those who labor in the word and teaching, and necessary to those who would acquit themselves like men, in every department of the

ranks of the great army of the Lord of Hosts, page
338.

And is not the conversion of the world and our
own eternal salvation infinitely worthy of all the
effort and enterprise in man, seeing God himself
has done so much in the gift of his Son and Holy
Spirit, and left for us so little to do–nothing,
indeed, but what is in the compass of our power?

Rise up, then, in the strength of Judah's Lion! Be
valiant for the truth! Adorn yourselves with all the
graces of the Spirit of God! Put on the armor of
light; and with all the gentleness, and meekness,
and mildness there is in Christ–with all the
courage, and patience and zeal, and effort, worthy
of a cause so salutary, so pure, so holy, and so
divine, determine never to faint nor to falter till
you enter the pearly gates-never to lay down your
arms till, with the triumphant millions, you stand
before the throne, and exultingly sing, "Worthy is
the Lamb that was slain, to receive power, and
riches, and wisdom, and might, and honor, and
glory, and blessing!" "To Him who sits upon the
throne, and to the Lamb, be blessing, and honor,
and glory, and strength, forever and forever!"
Amen. Page 339.

WALTER SCOTT. In the *Christian Baptist,* June 4,
1827, writing under the name "Philip," Walter Scott wrote the
second in a series called *On Experimental Religion.* In that
article he said:

In the law Jews sin against his moral authority,
expressed on tables; but in the gospel, in which

God has substituted spirit for literal sounds and
natural symbols, the worshiper sin against the Holy
Spirit, they grieve or quench the Holy Spirit, for
the gospel is the ministration of Spirit. In the first
dispensation, we see; in the second, we hear; in the
last we enjoy God. But how the uncreated Spirit
dwells in a created spirit, filling it with joy, we
know not; but certain it is that this fellowship is set
forth in the following words: Revelation 3:20;
John 14:21. Supping with Christ means joy in a
holy spirit ... But some will say, When is this gift
of the Holy Spirit given-before or after belief? In
reference to this good gift of God, I heard it
observed a few nights ago that we had turned the
gospel wrong end foremost-the modern gospel
reading thus: "Unless you receive the Spirit you
cannot believe!" The ancient gospel reading thus:
Unless you believe you cannot receive the Holy
Spirit; or to give it in the terms of Peter, "Believe
and be baptized and you shall receive the gift of
the Holy Spirit, for the promise (i.e. of the Holy
Spirit) is to you," etc. etc... Ye cavilers, ye
conceited few, who boast of your scriptural
knowledge,- but whose spirits, nevertheless, cannot
move even the elements of the heavenly oracles, let
me whisper to you a secret, that the kingdom of
heaven is not so much in an abundant knowledge,
as in an abundant spirit of righteousness, peace and
holy joy.

Walter Scott's crowning work was a treatise entitled, *The
Gospel Restored. A Discourse of The True Gospel of Jesus*

*Christ, In Which The Facts, Principles, Duties, and Privileges
of Christianity Are Arranged, Defined, and Discussed, And The
Gospel In Its Various Parts Shown To Be Adapted To The
Nature and Necessities Of Man In His Present Condition.*
Several sections of this book are well worth citing.

> One of the sweetest and most endearing ideas
> which our beloved Lord communicated concerning
> the Holy Spirit, is that he would, when he came, be
> a substitute for him in the church, and comfort his
> people throughout all ages while they mourned for
> the world, and worshiped an absent Lord . . . He
> was to be a substitute for our all-merciful but
> absent Lord ... With me it's a serious belief that if
> the church had been left with but faith and
> forgiveness and the effects of them upon the souls
> and lives of the disciples, excellent and precious
> though they be, she should still have felt forlorn; "I
> will not leave you forlorn"; But receiving this
> inestimable gift, if it lifts her head not on high to
> that happy holy place honored and glorified by the
> personal presence of our God and his Son down to
> her and fills her bosom with joys unutterable and
> full of glory . . . Is our Redeemer on high? By his
> Holy Spirit he is also in our hearts. Is he infinitely
> great? He is also infinitely condescending, and
> while he fills heaven, and the heaven of heavens,
> he dwells also in these poor bosoms of ours! Do
> the myriads of heavenly angels behold him? By his
> Spirit we more than behold him, we taste of his
> blessedness; we feed on him as on the bread of
> heaven, and feel that he is in us as a well of water

springing up unto everlasting life . . . *I will send him to you,* – Here then is a promise of a great missionary from on high, the Holy Spirit, to whom was committed the cause and comfort of the saints in all ages, pages 519-521.

The idea of the Spirit's being a missionary to the church, affords a new and striking argument against that immoral and fatal maxim in popular theology, namely, that special spiritual operations are necessary to faith! In this discourse it is shown that the church was formed before any of her members received the Spirit; . . . finally, that men did not and do not receive the Spirit to make them disciples, but because they were or are disciples; in a word it is shown, from the express words of Christ himself, that no man that does not first of all believe the gospel can receive the Holy Spirit. If any man thirst, says Christ, let him come unto me and drink, and out of his belly shall flow rivers of living waters. Now what does this mean; that the Holy Spirit will be given to unbelievers? No! John the Apostle explains it as follows: "This he spake of the Spirit which was to be given to those who believed, for the Spirit was not yet given (to believers) because Jesus was not yet glorified." Page 528.

Here, then, we have the descent of the great spiritual missionary into the body of Christ, the church; from which moment he has never left it, and never can leave it; for while the personal mission of Jesus to the Jews, and of the Apostles to the world were only temporary, the mission of the Holy Spirit into the body of Christ is perpetual and will end only at the resurrection (read Romans 8:11). If it be asked why there is no instance of supplication, deprecation, thanksgiving, prayer, or praise being offered to the Holy Spirit in the Scriptures, I answer that the Holy Spirit being in the church, all saints are represented as offering these spiritual sacrifices to God, through Jesus Christ, by the Holy Spirit which dwells in them. Hence the Spirit sheds abroad God's love in our hearts, groans, helps our infirmities, and makes intercession for the saints. And when the whole church shall be gathered home, there will be seen in heaven this wonderful spectacle the church glorified by the Holy Spirit, into which she had been baptized: the Son at her head, by whom she had been redeemed; and God on his throne, whom she had worshiped and adored ... But mark, reader, that there is no member of the body of Christ in whom the Holy Spirit dwelleth not; for it will hold as good at the end of the world as it does now, and it holds as good now as it did on the day of Pentecost and afterwards, that "if any man have not the Spirit of Christ he is none of his." Pages 535-536.

The use made of the Apostle's analogy (1 Corinthians 12, the body of Christ) is, I hope, strictly proper; and the whole affords a fine argument against the popular error concerning the Spirit that makes him go into a body that is not his; and bids the world hope to receive him before they become members of the church by faith and immersion. This discourse is to inculcate the great truth, that the Spirit is given to every one who becomes a member, but to no one in order to make him a member, Footnote Page 538.

1. Has the Spirit which was sent down from heaven on the day of Pentecost ever left his body? No; never. A human body without the spirit is dead; and Christ's body (the church) without the Spirit in her would be dead also. He shall abide with you forever.

2. Can he be in any person that is not of the body? No, he dwells in the saints; and as well might we hope for a man's spirit to occupy a space beyond his person, as for the Spirit of Christ to be found outside his body.

3. How does the Spirit of Christ operate? As our spirits operate in our bodies and by their members, so the Spirit of Christ operates in the body of Christ and its members.

4. Finally, how may a man possess himself of the Spirit of Christ? God has appointed a means of communicating every blessing in nature and in religion. He gives us fruit from the tree; water from the fountain; corn from the soil; and wines from the grape. Join yourself, then, to the body of Christ, and you will receive the Spirit of Christ. How am I to do this? If you believe in Christ, and think that God means what he says, I would

venture to quote my text as an infallible direction how you may receive the Spirit: "Repent and be baptized, every one of you, in the name of the Lord Jesus Christ, for the remission of sins, and ye shall receive the gift of the Holy Spirit." Does this please you? Then obey the Lord. Page 538-539.

LARD'S QUARTERLY. Moses Lard started a paper in September of 1863 in which many essays on the Holy Spirit and His influences in the world were discussed. This paper had an excellent spirit of controversy in the attitude of love. Several essays in this publications are worthy of quoting.

Moses Lard: Being now through with stating preliminaries, I proceed to make an application of them to the position or doctrine which it is the more especial object of this article to defend. That position is this: *That the Holy Spirit dwells in Christians.* (He then cites as proof Romans 8:11 and 1 Corinthians 6:19, RR) . . . In what sense must we take the clause, "which dwelleth in you?" To this inquiry we have two different replies involving two opposite theories.

The first is, that we are to take the clause literally; and hence to hold that the Holy Spirit actually and literally dwells in Christians.

The second is, that we are to take the clause not literally but figuratively; and hence to hold that the Holy Spirit dwells in Christians not actually and literally but representatively or through the truth.

But what kind of dwelling is this last? Let the language be understood. When it is said that the Holy

Spirit dwells in Christians not actually and literally, but merely through the truth or representatively, the implication clearly is, *that the Spirit itself does not dwell in them at all.* On the contrary, *the truth only* dwells in them, and this stands for or is in the place of the Spirit. This unquestionably is the meaning of the language. Which now of these two theories are we to accept as the correct one? Of course the answer must depend on the acceptation in which we take the clause, "dwells in you." In what sense are we to take it?

The rule by which the answer to this question is to be determined is this: A word, whenever met with, is to be taken in its common current sense, unless the subject-matter, the context, or a qualifying epithet forbids it. This rule is universal and imperative. What the phrase "dwells in" means is perfectly clear; namely, to live in or inhabit as a home. This, then, in the sense in which we must take the clause, unless prevented as the rule requires. Now, as to a qualifying epithet there is none; and a glance of the eye at the context is enough to satisfy us that there is nothing in it to prevent the clause being taken in its common acceptation. The only item, then, remaining to be considered is the subject-matter.

But what is this? The subject of the sentence in hand is, *the Holy Spirit,* the thing said of it, *that it dwells in Christians;* and these together constitute the subject-matter or the thought presented in the sentence for consideration. Now if the subject-matter involves anything to prevent the clause being taken in its ordinary sense, it must be the Spirit itself. Does the Spirit itself, then, prevent it? and if so on account of what?

1st. It cannot be on account of anything in its nature, For of the nature of substance of the Spirit, strictly speaking, we know nothing. Of course, then, we cannot affirm that it is such as to prevent the Spirit dwelling in Christians. From this source, therefore, nothing can be deduced forbidding the clause being taken in its usual sense.

2nd. It cannot be on account of its inability or want of power. Surely no one will deny that the Spirit dwells in Christians on the score it cannot. We know of no limits to its power; hence we must use no language which implies any.

3rd. Nor can it be because it *will not*. To assert this would be presumptuous indeed. We know nothing to justify it; neither does the word of God teach it. It is hence inadmissible.

4th. Neither can it be owing to anything in the office of the Spirit in the work of redemption. For all we know of office we learn from holy writ; and it is simply certain that we learn nothing there against the notion that the Spirit dwells in Christians; and hence nothing to forbid the clause being taken in its usual sense.

But without being more lengthy, I feel safe in concluding that we know of nothing respecting the Spirit to prevent the clause in question being taken in its common current acceptation. Of course an arbitrary meaning is out of the question. I hence decide that the clause, "dwells in you," is to be taken it its ordinary literal sense. To this conclusion we are absolutely tied down by the preceding law of exegesis. We could not reject it if we would.

From all of which it follows that the assertion: "the Spirit dwells in you," cannot be taken in any other than a literal current sense. Therefore that the Holy Spirit actually and literally dwells in Christians is indisputably affirmed in the word of God; and hence cannot be rejected.

But in reply to all this we shall be told that God is said to dwell in Christians (2 Corinthians 6:16), that this is not a literal, but representative indwelling, that is, a dwelling "through the Spirit" (Ephesians 2:22); and that consequently in this sense must we regard the Holy Spirit as dwelling in Christians.

This is the strong, and I believe regarded as the decisive, refutatory argument of those who deny a literal indwelling of the Holy Spirit. It is proper therefore to subject it to a severe examination. In the first place, then, I admit its promises and deny its conclusion. In other words I admit, first, that God dwells in Christians; and, second, that this dwelling is not literal but through the Spirit. But on what ground is this admission made? Simply on the ground that the word of God actually asserts what is admitted. But can we grant so much respecting the case of the Holy Spirit, and on the same ground? Not at all. For though the Holy Spirit is certainly said to dwell in Christians;

it is not said to dwell in them through something else.
Hence one of the things which is said of God is not
said of the Holy Spirit, and this is *the very thing* in
issue. The difference, therefore, between the two cases
is the difference between an actual assertion of holy
writ, and in a mere inference of the human mind. If it
were anywhere asserted in the Bible that the Holy
Spirit dwells in Christians through the truth, through
faith, or through anything else, no one need contend
for a literal indwelling. An epithet qualifying the
phrase, "dwells in," in one place, might, I think, be
fairly assumed to qualify it in every place.

But such an epithet we have not; and certainly it
would be a most dangerous procedure to assume it.

Had the Bible said that God dwells in Christians,
without an epithet qualifying the phrase, dwells in,
then by every law of interpretation known to the
learned world should we have been compelled to
assert a literal indwelling. Now what in that case we
should have been compelled to do, I hold that in this
we are compelled to do. The Bible says that the Holy
Spirit dwells in Christians; and this indwelling is no
where qualified by an epithet. We are thus compelled
to believe it literal. But why? Can this question be
answered on any other ground than this: That
inspiration itself designed to make a difference
between the indwelling of God and that of the Spirit?
One thing is certain, a deep difference is inscribed on
the verbiage of the two cases; and this with me is con-
clusive that a corresponding difference exists in the
facts described.

But the proposition, that God dwells in Christians not literally but through the Spirit, instead, it seems to me, of disproving that the Spirit dwells literally in them, establishes it. For how can God dwell in Christians through the Spirit if the Spirit itself does not dwell in them? When men say that the Spirit dwells in Christians through the truth, they claim for the truth a literal indwelling; yet when God is said to dwell in them through the Spirit, they deny of the Spirit a literal indwelling. Are they consistent?

But why should any one doubt that the Holy Spirit dwells literally in Christians? It cannot be on the ground that it is not clearly enough asserted. Still by some it is doubted, and we repeat, why? Is it on the ground of our inability to comprehend and explain the fact and mode of such indwelling? We fear that this has much to do with the case. But is this a legitimate ground of doubt? In some case it is, I grant, but not in this. Such is the nature of the fact asserted that we cannot comprehend it. This we are compelled to confess. Now instead of this inability being a just ground of doubt, it seems to me that it should be just the reverse. For the more sensible we feel that we cannot and do not comprehend a fact, the less reason we have to question what the Bible says concerning it. Of all the possible grounds upon which a doubt might be founded, this should be the last.

Surely a literal indwelling is not doubted on the ground that we have no *sensible* evidence of the Spirit's presence. For neither *a priori* nor from the Bible have we any reason to conclude that such evidence would be afforded us. And gratuitously to assume it, and then make the assumption a ground on which to doubt the indwelling, is most unwarrantable indeed.

But it is perhaps doubted on the score that we have no conscious evidence of any emotions excited within us by the Spirit. I cannot admit it. I am distinctly conscious at this instant of the presence in my mind of a love, joy, and peace, or exquisite sweetness, as I am of the purpose to end the sentence I am now writing; and these are called in the word of God "the fruit of the Spirit." But as a rejoinder to this we may be told that men who are acknowledged not to have the Spirit, are no less vividly conscious of the same emotions. I positively deny it. That they have at times a love, a joy, a peace of a certain kind, I grant; but they are not the broad love, the ineffable joy, and the deep unperturbable peace of the Christian. Only one thing more need be added here, that we are never conscious of an emotion *as from* the Spirit. Consciousness avouches only the emotion, the Bible announces whence it is.

From all of the foregoing, therefore, it appears that we have no just ground on which to deny the literal indwelling of the Spirit. Hence such indwelling must be accepted as the clear authoritative teaching of holy writ. If this conclusion be not legitimate and fair I confess my inability to conceive the circumstances which could render it so.

We need the Holy Spirit, then, to strengthen us with might in the inner man; we need it to help our infirmities, we need it to intercede for us, we need it to groan within us, to groan when the brain has ceased to work save in stupor or delirium, to groan when the lip is stiff and the tongue still, to groan in life's last agony, to groan for the soul as it floats out with the last breath and spreads its wings for home–we need it then. O! deliver me from the cold material philosophy which denies that God has placed within me a comforter, a strengthener. I cling to the belief as I do the shreds that knit my heart together. Volume 1, Pages 234-241.

J.W. McGarvey: Commenting on 1 Corinthians 12:13, "The term *drink* certainly expresses the idea of receiving within us what is drunk; and when used of the Holy Spirit it is scarcely possible that it does not refer to the reception of the Spirit within us. Volume 1, Page 438.

Thomas Munnell: Here we close our review of this long essay by Bro. Christopher. It is a good thing while men often fall below their theory, they frequently are better than their theory. I am happy to know that while some are even less orthodox than the essay before us, denying the communion of the Holy Spirit altogether, not even admitting his being *among* us except by the word, they nevertheless have the love of God shed abroad in their hearts by the Holy Spirit, although they think it is all done by the word. In the case before us, the writer is evidently in advance of his theory, as the spirit and mellow tone of his elegantly written production plainly indicates. The theory itself, however, would ultimately tend to cheapen religion in the hearts of the people. The tendency of men at best is to shallowness in their religious experience, and every member of the church should be taught to keep the temple of his own body pure and sanctified for the indwelling Spirit of God. To every brother we would kindly say: Try to enjoy the love of God, the grace of the Lord Jesus Christ, and the communion of the Holy Spirit. Volume 4, Page 28.

J.W. McGARVEY: All of McGarvey's books were written by the year 1892 when he published the *New Commentary on Acts*. We will notice several quotations from several of his books.

> The second blessing promised on condition of repentance and baptism, is the "gift of the Holy Spirit." By this is not meant that miraculous gift which had just been bestowed upon the apostles; for we know from all subsequent history that this gift was not bestowed on all who repented and were baptized, but on only a few brethren of prominence in the several congregations. The expression means the Holy Spirit as a gift; and the reference is that indwelling of the Holy Spirit by which we bring forth the fruits of the Spirit, and without which we are not of Christ. Of this promise Peter speaks more fully in the next sentence of his sermon. *New Commentary on Acts,* Page 39, commenting on Acts 2:38.

Now he that wrought us for this very thing is God, who gave unto us the earnest of the Spirit (2 Cor. 5:5). God designed man for such super-investment, and hence placed in him the longing that should be satisfied, he has given us of his own Spirit, it is a light thing that he should give us the spiritual body (Romans 8:32). *Commentary on 2 Corinthians*, Page 193.

Jesus removed this obstructing law and curse, that in himself he might bring Abraham's blessing of justification upon the Gentiles, that all might receive the fulfillment of God's promise, that promise which agreed to give the Spirit to all who rendered the obedience of faith–Acts 2:38-39. _Commentary on Galatians_, Page 267 (Galatians 3:14).

Because the love which God has for him fills his heart, being inwardly manifested to him by the Holy Spirit, who is given to all believers–at the time of their regeneration. Commentary on Romans 5:5, Page 331.

We may look for him (God) to raise us from the dead by the indwelling Holy Spirit, just as he raised Christ from the dead by the same indwelling Spirit. Commentary on Romans 8:11, Page 359-360.

The Spirit knows these needful things, and he affords a remedy for our weakness by himself interceding for us, not praying independently, or apart from us, but moving and exalting us in our prayer, and stirring within us sighings, longings, aspirations and soulful yearnings for those things which are our real needs, but which are so poorly understood by us that we cannot adequately express them in words. Commentary on Romans 8:26-27, Page 365.

R.L. WHITESIDE: In the year 1932 brother Whiteside printed in the Gospel Advocate several articles on various facets of the doctrine of the Holy Spirit. In Doctrinal Discourses these have been reprinted. The following quotations

are from the one entitled *The Indwelling of the Holy Spirit*
Pages 196-199.

> I have heard this argument on the setting up on the
> church before Pentecost, though it never did seem to
> me to be conclusive: "The church is a body; and if it
> was set up before the Spirit was given on Pentecost, it
> was a body without a Spirit, and a body without a
> spirit is dead." And the one who made the argument
> was likely to deny that the Spirit now dwells in the
> church! Is the church now a dead body? Think on
> these things. "And we are witnesses of these things;
> and so is the Holy Spirit, whom God hath given to
> them that obey him" (Acts 5:32). Have you obeyed
> God? One good brother said, "I know I haven't the
> Holy Spirit in me; if I had I could feel it." A
> denominationalist rises up in meeting and says, "I
> know I have the Holy Spirit, for I can feel it." So there
> you are both depend on their feelings as evidence.
>
> In such talk God's word is ruled out of court. Is not
> that so? "Or know ye not that your body is a temple of
> the Holy Spirit which is in you, which ye have from
> God" (1 Cor. 6:19). Not by feelings, but only by
> revelation, may we know this. I do not even feel my
> own spirit, neither do I know much about how it
> dwells in my body. I think I know my spirit is not in
> the food I eat, and I know that if I do not eat food, my
> spirit will leave my body. The word of God is the
> Christian's food. You can follow up the analogy, and
> yet the analogy may not be conclusive proof to you.
> "But if the Spirit of him that raised up Jesus from the
> dead dwelleth in you, he that raised up Jesus Christ

from the dead shall give life also to your mortal
bodies through His Spirit that dwelleth in you"
(Romans 8:11).

But I have been met with this statement: "The Holy
Spirit dwells in us, just as Christ does–by faith." –
"That Christ may dwell in your hearts through faith"
(Eph. 3:17). And it also said that we are justified by
faith (Romans 5:1). In both cases is not faith the
condition? On that condition the facts stated are
based–faith is the condition, not a substitute for the
thing affirmed–Justification or Christ. Jesus said, "I
will not leave you desolate (margin, orphans): I come
unto you" (John 14:18). He would come to them in
the person of the Holy Spirit (John 14:16-17). Again
he says, verse 23: "If a man love me he will keep my
word: and my Father will love him and we will come
unto him, and make our abode with him." Does this
mean anything to you? Jesus and the Father are so
closely united that he could say, "I and the Father are
one" (John 10:30). And after the Spirit came, the
Father and the Son act through the agency of the
Spirit. Hence Paul could say of Christ the Lord and
God, ". . . in whom each several building, fitly framed
together, groweth into a holy temple in the Lord: in
whom ye also are builded together for a habitation of
God in the Spirit" (Eph. 2:21-22).

What does the indwelling Spirit do? What if I am
unable to answer that question? And what if no one
else can give a definite answer, would our inability to
answer the question nullify what God has said? If we
cannot explain a thing, shall we say there is no such

thing? Let us not jump to unwarranted conclusions. This we do when we say, that if the Holy Spirit really dwelt in us, we could speak by inspiration and work miracles. John was filled with the Spirit from his mother's womb (Luke 1:15). 1 hardly think anyone will say that John worked miracles and spoke by inspiration in his mother's womb. And he never did work any miracles, even though he was a prophet (John 10:41). If an apostle were living today, I feel sure he could not speak by inspiration or work a miracle. The whole plan of salvation has been fully revealed, confirmed and recorded; no additional revelations are needed. But let us think of one idea that has been with me for years. Did you, brother preacher, ever pray for the Lord to lead you into the places where you can do the most good? No? Well, you should; the Lord knows you and he knows the fields, and he therefore knows where you can do the most good. You do not know. For a long time I have prayed for the Lord to lead me into places where I could do the most good. Why not?

To these could be added many others from men living and dead. The citing of these does not mean that the writer agrees with everything quoted. And I am sure that the men quoted would not agree with every conclusion of this writer. I am grateful for the fact that good men have written for my edification the fruit of their study and wisdom.

CPSIA information can be obtained
at www.ICGtesting.com
Printed in the USA
BVHW082136201219
566948BV00005B/24/P